NUMEROLOGY

RODFORD BARRAT is a highly respected numerologist who lectures widely on how to improve life by the use of numbers. His work on numerology has been translated into many languages and sold throughout the world. He has contributed articles to various magazines and researched the ancient link between colour and the name, and the metaphysical effect of sound.

THE SERIES

New Perspectives provide attractive and accessible introductions to a comprehensive range of mind, body and spirit topics. Beautifully designed and illustrated, these practical books are written by experts in each subject.

Titles in the series include:

ALEXANDER TECHNIQUE
by Richard Brennan

MASSAGE
by Stewart Mitchell

AROMATHERAPY
by Christine Wildwood

MEDITATION
by David Fontana

DREAMS
by David Fontana

NLP
by Carol Harris

FENG SHUI
by Man-Ho Kwok with Joanne O'Brien

NUMEROLOGY
by Rodford Barrat

FLOWER REMEDIES
by Christine Wildwood

REFLEXOLOGY
by Inge Dougans

HOMEOPATHY
by Peter Adams

TAROT
by A T Mann

New Perspectives

NUMEROLOGY

An Introductory Guide to the Power of Numbers as a Guide for Life

RODFORD BARRAT

ELEMENT

Shaftesbury, Dorset • Boston, Massachusetts
Melbourne, Victoria

First published as *The Elements of Numerology*
in 1994 by Element Books Limited

This revised edition first published in Great Britain in
1999 by Element Books Limited
Shaftesbury, Dorset SP7 8BP

Published in the USA in 1999 by
Element Books, Inc.
160 North Washington Street,
Boston, MA 02114

Published in Australia in 1999 by
Element Books and distributed by
Penguin Australia Limited
487 Maroondah Highway,
Ringwood, Victoria 3134

Designed for Element Books Limited by
Design Revolution, Queens Park Villa,
30 West Drive, Brighton, East Sussex BN2 2GE

ELEMENT BOOKS LIMITED
Editorial Director: Sarah Sutton
Editorial Manager: Jane Pizzey
Commissioning Editor: Grace Cheetham
Production Director: Roger Lane

DESIGN REVOLUTION
Editorial Director: Ian Whitelaw
Art Director: Lindsey Johns
Editor: Martin Bryant
Designer: Vanessa Good

Printed and bound in Great Britain by
Bemrose Security Printing, Derby

British Library Cataloguing in Publication
data available

Library of Congress Cataloging in Publication
data available

ISBN 1-86204-625-5

CONTENTS

Acknowledgements

A big thank you to Dorothy Price who has encouraged me all my life. Thanks to Rodney James, Corrine Squire, Alan Bird, Margie Kelly, Keith Mayle, Margaret Marsden Travers, Marie Jelliman, Paco Sirvent, Robert Hollander, Romy Hammes Mowbray and Jill Petrovitch McHugh. Thanks also to everyone at Element Books Limited, and last but not least, to Doreen Montgomery of Rupert Crew.

For Lilian

INTRODUCTION

CHAPTER ONE

The whole heaven is a musical scale and number.

ARISTOTLE

Numbers can speak. Their language is numerology: an ancient science that is a numerical analysis of life – your life. It is a practical system that can be used today; it helps the unfolding of spiritual insight and the attainment of material success. This sounds like the stuff of fortune tellers' dreams but the reason a belief in the power of numbers has existed for thousands of years is because it works. It is possible to prove this for yourself.

Numerology shows your motivation; it reveals your talents; it displays how you appear to other people. It maps the trends of each day: what is happening, what has happened, and why. It indicates what is to come. Using this language of numbers improves the quality of life spiritually, emotionally, mentally or materially.

'Have you the grass that sings or the bird that is blue?' asks a character in *The Blue Bird*, a play by the Belgian writer, Maurice Maeterlinck. A search is made for this bird. Finally, it is found at home in its cage. It had been there all the time. The blue bird symbolizes happiness. Numerology shows, using numbers as symbols, how you can find your blue bird. You already have it. The numbers hidden inside your birthdate and name reveal your opportunities, abilities and talents. Knowledge of these symbols can create a happier life. Numerology is one of the simplest metaphysical systems to learn and this guide enables you to compile your own numerological chart.

NUMEROLOGY AND PLACES

In numerology, cities, countries and towns have numbers assigned to their names. America vibrates to the number 5 and anyone with a 5 prominent in his or her chart would find living in America would further their aims. Great Britain vibrates to a 7 and Australia to a 3. These are generalizations. Yet, surprisingly, the vibrations of the numbers support the national stereotypes. Five seeks freedom, 7 is reserved, and 3 is a friendly, sociable number.

Everything in the universe vibrates, and by using numbers – in the form of metaphysical arithmetic – we apply these vibrations as numbers to people, their names, their lives. Each number is a symbol that represents certain qualities. This is what this ancient belief or science is based upon.

ABOVE THIS ANCIENT GRID OF NUMBERS FROM 1 TO 9 ADDS UP TO THE NUMBER 15 HORIZONTALLY, VERTICALLY OR DIAGONALLY.

The Chinese, the Egyptians, the Chaldeans, Greeks and Romans have all used their own numerological systems. The Chinese I Ching, which is thought to be over 4000 years old, states that odd numbers are light and even numbers dark. The Kabala, a system of ancient Jewish mysticism, reveals spiritual truths through its use of number, letter and sound. The Tarot also has numerological symbolism attached to it; and there is an old system of divination that uses numbers called Arithmancy.

The main system in use today, and the one described in this book, is called Modern Numerology, or Pythagorean Numerology, and it is supposedly based on the teachings of the Greek mathematician and philosopher, Pythagoras, who lived in the sixth century BC.

NUMEROLOGY TODAY

The 'birth' of our present-day numerological system and the beginning of its popularity is credited to an American woman, Mrs L. Dow Balliet. In the early part of the twentieth century she wrote two books equating the traditional symbolism of numbers with the English alphabet. Her system was later refined and popularized by other numerologists, Dr Julia Seton being among the most prominent.

In *The Secrets of Numbers*, published in 1963, Lionel Stebbing writes: 'Numbers are not the cause of events but they illustrate the order and measure that is inherent in life.'

Previously, odd numbers were regarded as active or masculine, even numbers as passive or feminine – this can be related to the light and dark numbers of the I Ching. Today, we often find the emphasis of light/active given to masculine associations and dark/passive given to feminine as objectionable.

Generally, the odd numbers are solo performers and the even numbers work at their best with others (the number 8 is a possible exception to this generalization). The nine numbers represent the following qualities:

LEFT ODD AND EVEN NUMBERS HAVE, IN THE PAST, BEEN SEEN AS HAVING ACTIVE AND PASSIVE ASPECTS, LIKE THE LIGHT AND DARK SIDES OF THE TAOIST YIN-YANG SYMBOL.

THE NINE NUMBERS

1 Leadership. Initiative. Originality. Determination.

2 Cooperation. Diplomacy. Friendship. Kindness.

3 Self-expression. Creativity. Joy. Laughter.

4 Practicality. Self-discipline. Stability. Work.

5 Freedom. Communication. Versatility. Sensuality.

6 Harmony. Creativity. Responsibility. Domesticity.

7 Individuality. Intuition. Perfection. Contemplation.

8 Power. Independence. Ambition. Organization.

9 Compassion. Idealism. Great drama. Romanticism.

The zero is not considered in conventional numerology, although when lying behind a number it magnifies the qualities of that number. In Indian numerology it is often considered unfortunate.

It is enjoyable to classify people according to their Life Path Number, which is found in their birthdate (see Chapter 2), and although all the numbers should be considered together, to illustrate the main qualities of the numbers we will use as examples nine people whose public personas seem to match their single most important number, their Life Path.

FAMOUS PEOPLE

Life Path 1 Mikhail
  Gorbachev

Life Path 2 Bill Clinton

Life Path 3 Bill Cosby

Life Path 4 Margaret
  Thatcher

Life Path 5 Mick Jagger

Life Path 6 Federico Fellini

Life Path 7 Diana, Princess
  of Wales

Life Path 8 Elizabeth Taylor

Life Path 9 Mahatma Gandhi

This, while interesting, should not be taken too seriously. Considering one number by itself is the same as judging someone by their sun sign in astrology, when the position of all the planets should be considered.

THE QUALITIES OF THE AGE

For the past one thousand years, the number 1 has held the dominant position. Each year has begun with 1. The 1 is associated with the masculine principle: the desire to lead, the desire to dominate.

We now enter a new age – the number 2 takes up the position held by 1. The 2 has stood for cooperation, sensitivity and friendship and has been associated with women (because of this it has sometimes been considered a negative number – by men). It is no coincidence, when we consider the numbers, that the rise in the power of women – the feminist movement – has occurred as the number 2 takes over (2000 AD). The increasing awareness of the rights of other species, green issues, the conservation of land – all these movements are reflected in the change of the date. Numerology shows that it is a New Age beginning. The Age of the 2.

11

RIGHT THE NUMBER 2 IS ASSOCIATED WITH WOMEN AND SENSITIVITY.

FOLLOWING THE YEAR 2000 THE POWER OF THE 2 WILL INCREASE..

The past century, the 19th, has shown the power that is generated by 1 and 9 together. The 9 reflects humanitarian values that have grown during the last hundred years – but 9 in its negative aspect symbolizes war and aggression. The 19 is known as a karmic number by some numerologists, signifying a battle for independence and a breaking away from past conditions. Naturally, the numbers of each decade will add their influence.

The Nineties represent endings, change, great drama and humanitarian values – all shown by the number 9. The Berlin Wall fell in 1989, the date of the year had two 9s, the 1 and the 8 added together also came to 9. Three 9s, while representing the potential for change and idealistic action, can create a severe disruptive influence. The Nineties reflected this in greater criminal activity in many countries and social and civil disobedience on the streets.

The Eighties were a time of increasing material wealth in the West – the era of the 'yuppy'. Eight is a powerful number, often associated with business and executive talents. It can make money (by working hard) but can become greedy. You can write down the number 8 over and over again, without taking your pen off the paper. From wherever you start, you return back to the same place. Whatever the 8 does, it gets back.

In the Seventies people liked to 'do their own thing'. It was the permissive age, a time for individualism. Number 7 people need to experience life for themselves. They have to make their own mistakes. They usually do.

The Sixties heralded 'flower power', 'make love, not war'. The 6 brings harmony, balance, and loves beauty and colour around it. This number reflected the ideals of the 'flower children' of the period. The influence of the 9 in front of the 6 – 1960s – brought many changes in the home, marriage and the upbringing of children.

In the Fifties, a need to feel free again took over and new and progressive changes occurred. It was a time of pushing against boundaries and an increased curiosity about the world after the restriction of the 4 of the Forties.

AMERICA AND THE NUMBER 7

The American Declaration of Independence, 7. 4. 1776, has three 7s – individuality, a dislike of being told what to do, a need to make its own mistakes – in the date, which also adds up numerologically (as you will discover) to the number 5. Five represents freedom, change, versatility. The name America also vibrates to this freedom seeking number, and the word 'independence' has seven of its twelve letters under the vibration of 5.

Predicting the future by numerology can never be 100 per cent accurate. The numbers reveal trends. A numerological forecast is no more special or mystical than predicting the weather or deciding on stock market trends, although often more accurate. It will be your informed opinion. There is nothing psychic about it. As you become used to using numbers, certain numerical spreads will reveal truths to you that less-informed eyes would overlook.

PERSONAL YEAR AND YOUR NAME

Two controversial areas in numerology deserve a mention. Some numerologists believe that the Personal Year, which shows the trends for each person for a period of 12 months, starts on the 1st of January of each year. Others believe it starts on a person's 'birthday'. I believe it is the former. You will be able, looking at past events in your own life, to form your own opinion.

Some numerologists believe the full name on the birth certificate (if you have one) is the only accurate guide to the influence of your name. Thus if 'Baby Girl' is written on your birth certificate, in place of the name that you were eventually known by, then Baby Girl is the name that you will analyse. Others believe if your name has influence it has to be the name that you are known by, the name you use. I am certain this latter view is correct.

The easy way to learn the elements of numerology is to analyse yourself and you can note the attributes of your own personal numbers as you go along. A pattern will emerge. It can take you by surprise.

In this book we begin by examining the numbers in your birthdate. These are important. They cannot be changed. The effect of your name comes next and influences what you want and how you carry out your plans. Finally we look at predictive numerology to see the trends in your life. There really is a right time, right place and right name.

A healthy approach to number analysis is to remember there are aspects of life that numbers will not show. Are you good looking or ugly? Were you born rich or poor? Were traditional beliefs instilled in you from an early age? Do you live in a cold or hot climate? All these, and more, influence our behaviour. They must be considered alongside your numerological profile.

14

Four Rules to Remember

1   Numbers have good and bad sides. They are symbols for positive and negative characteristics.

2   Each number is different not better, nor worse, than others (this is the popular view, although some numerologists regard 4 and 8 as unlucky).

3   People with the same numbers have similar potential to work with. That is all. They do not react in exactly the same way.

4   Always consider all the numbers together, their combined effect. You are never represented by one number, even if it appears many times in your chart.

THE LIFE PATH

CHAPTER TWO

Consciousness of our powers increases them.
VAUVENARGUES

Your Life Path Number is your most important number. It is found in your birthdate, and in numerology it is as important as your sun sign is in Western astrology. While you should consider all your numbers, your Life Path is the key to your whole chart. It is considered your 'lucky' number. Whether you can use its power easily depends on your supporting numbers. Following the direction of the Life Path makes life easier – ignoring it makes it hard. It shows your direction in life, the main opportunities you will attract, your talents and characteristics.

You will usually recognize the direction of this path. At times you may resist following it and refuse its opportunities. This is often the case if your Birthday Number (described in chapter 4) is a different number. When this occurs, you can face 'problems' until you get your life back on track.

The meaning of the Sanskrit word Dharma could describe the function of the Life Path: the path to follow that accords with your essential nature. Each Life Path Number represents characteristics that are more likely to be displayed with that Life Path.

To find your Life Path Number, add all the numbers in your birthdate together. Continue to add the total together until only one digit is left. This is the usual way to find the essence of numbers in numerology. It is called fadic addition. As an example, we will use the birthdate of the American civil rights leader, Martin Luther King. Note that in America it is the month that comes first in the date, while in Britain it is the day.

MARTIN LUTHER KING

Birthdate: 1. 15. 1929

$1 + 1 + 5 + 1 + 9 + 2 + 9 = 28$ $2 + 8 = 10$ $1 + 0 = 1$

Martin Luther King's Life Path Number is 1.

The Life Path is the direction in life, the main opportunities that occur, the important talents and abilities. Or, putting it another way, what you can do, what you should do, and what will come to you.

LIFE PATH 1   THE LEADER

Direction:	to learn to become self-reliant.
Opportunities:	to lead or initiate projects.
Keywords:	Leader. Initiator. Self-starter. Originator. Popular. Selfish. Egotistical. Dominating. Tyrant.

Ones have drive, determination and dash. They prefer to act rather than think. With their good concentration they can single-mindedly go after what they want. They want to do something rather than wait and they dislike sitting on the sidelines. Lack of patience is sometimes a problem. Often ambitious, with leadership ability, they can make instant decisions but dislike seeing them changed by someone else. Strong beliefs are combined with a forthright manner. They work best alone, although they are usually popular among their colleagues. In business they are self-assured with the ability to handle their own problems. Original, brave and courageous, they dislike meeting opposition and will avoid it if they can.

Negatively, they are never satisfied with what they achieve and can be impatient. They are puzzled by people who are naturally slow starters and have difficulty accepting criticism. They hate arguments and to avoid them may sometimes delay taking assertive action. This causes extreme frustration. In love, their determination to lead can desert them.

Life Path 1s that have shown the positive characteristics of leadership and courage are Mikhail Gorbachev and Lech Walesa.

LIFE PATH 2: THE COOPERATOR

Direction:	to learn how to cooperate.
Opportunities:	to work well in partnerships or in groups.
Keywords:	Cooperator. Friend. Diplomat. Inspired. Musical. Indecisive. Shy. Timid. Self-pitying.

Twos consider the feelings of others – sometimes before their own; they can let others take the credit that is their due. Although not natural leaders like 1s, they can lead but they like a strong partner beside them. They attract attention or celebrity in life. People are fascinated by the inspiration they communicate and they are masters or mistresses of timing and wait patiently until the time is right before proceeding. They dislike being

RIGHT LIFE PATH 2S OFTEN HAVE AN ACCURATE SENSE OF RHYTHM AND MUSICAL TALENT.

hurried and should resist being forced to work at a pace that is uncomfortable for them. A love of music or musical ability is often present as they possess an accurate sense of rhythm. They are excellent at work that requires attention to detail. Polite and courteous, 2s are natural diplomats, being able to see both points of view. They prefer to have a partner to share their lives with and can enjoy working in a team. Natural collectors and hoarders, they usually enjoy hunting around markets.

Negatively, they have difficulty in making decisions as they dislike upsetting anyone. Sensitive and easily hurt, they can daydream too much. They can prefer to live out their fantasies in their minds rather than take action. Shyness or timidity can be a problem and they are uncomfortable if situations become too competitive.

Presidents Ronald Reagan and Bill Clinton are Life Path 2s, both appearing to have strong supportive partners. Singers Diana Ross and Shirley Bassey show 2's innate musicality.

LIFE PATH 3: THE ENTERTAINER

Direction: to learn how to create happiness.
Opportunities: to use creativity and imagination.
Keywords: Self-expressive. Gregarious. Creative. Lucky. Love-of-life. Vain. Restless. Easily bored. Jealous.

Threes are happy, enthusiastic bringers of joy. They light up the room. Imaginative, colourful people with creative ability, they have a natural wit and learn skills easily and quickly. There is a definite need for love in their lives. Many dancers are born with this Life Path and there is an attraction towards laughter, entertainment and the lighter side of life. They appear to be lucky people – they do make money easily. Something always seems to turn up for 3s. Eloquent and resilient, they are good hosts who enjoy being surrounded by people. They need to express their undoubted creativity in some way.

Negatively, they quickly become bored and restless. Although attracting money, they spend freely. They have trouble coping alone and fear being by themselves. Endurance is not one of their strengths and they need to pace themselves more.

The 3's gift of providing laughter is shown by the comedian Bill Cosby, and creative entertainment of a different sort by the film director Alfred Hitchcock. The 'life of the party' image could be attributed to the film actress Jayne Mansfield and the writer F. Scott Fitzgerald.

LIFE PATH 4: THE BUILDER

Direction: to build a life on solid foundations.
Opportunities: to use self-discipline constructively.
Keywords: Practical. Honest. Realistic. Orthodox. Hard-working. Loyal. Narrow-minded. Dogmatic. Dull.

Fours are practical people who will work hard to accomplish what they want. Serious, mature, with an organized way of doing things, they enjoy working to a plan. They push themselves and can work long hours. Life for them gets easier as they mature. The word 'foursquare' – solidly-based and steady – describes their lives. They are constructive and like to build solid foundations. There is often an ability to work with their hands. They are dependable, loyal and sincere. Security is important to them; they are unlikely to spend all of their money.

Orthodox thinkers who dislike diverging from their plans, they can be slow making decisions. When they feel secure they will take a risk, but not before. Negatively, they are workaholics, never knowing when to rest. Early life can be difficult. An original approach to a problem can scare them. They fear the new and at times their thinking becomes rigid and dogmatic.

Life Path 4 has featured among British Prime Ministers Margaret Thatcher, Harold Wilson and John Major. The actors Clint Eastwood and Arnold Schwarzenegger show the conventional strength of the Life Path 4 persona.

LIFE PATH 5: THE COMMUNICATOR

Direction: to learn to seek freedom.
Opportunities: to communicate and create change.
Keywords: Communicator. Freedom-seeker. Versatile.
                    Adaptable. Sexual. Quick-thinking. Analytical.
                    Progressive. Procrastinating. Love of pleasure.
                    Changing too often.

Five is the number of the senses, and these people radiate an unconscious sexual magnetism. They need to be free and will react quickly if they feel they are being manipulated. A love of change, progression and anything new typifies this number. They are instantly adaptable, multi-talented and need to use their versatility. They have an exciting and youthful attitude.

This is a physical number with a liking for competitive situations. They work well under stress. They do not possess 'team spirit', but hide this from others. Popular with both sexes, 5s can communicate to all types of people and can be brilliant sales people – mentally quick and eloquent.

They will seek a faster way to do things. With a love of travel they can easily live out of a suitcase. Curious about others, shrewd and analytical, 5s see other people as they are and have no trouble accepting them like that. They want to succeed and dislike failing but find it hard to accept help.

Negatively, they are self-indulgent and lack patience. They can, when unbalanced, indulge themselves in the 'sex, drugs and drink' lifestyle. They take too many risks and frequently change jobs or become so absorbed in a career or project, emotionally or mentally, they find it impossible to let go and change.

The 5's natural sexuality and avant-garde approach can be seen in Marlon Brando (acting); Mick Jagger (singing); Andre Agassi (tennis); and Rudolf Nureyev (dancing by leaping to freedom). The darker side of 5's popularity may be seen in Adolf Hitler.

LIFE PATH 6: THE TEACHER

Direction:	to learn the joys of responsibility.
Opportunities:	to be creative and create harmony.
Keywords:	Harmonious. Creative. Well-balanced.
	Responsible. Just. Advisor. Fair. Meddlesome.
	Anxious.

Sixes need a well-balanced life and constantly seek harmony and appreciate beautiful surroundings. They enjoy working in partnerships and function well as part of a team. Responsible, they take positions of trust seriously and responsibility is often thrust upon them. They dislike unfairness and love fair play. Extremely loyal, similar to 4 in this respect, they make friends for life. Needing a peaceful home life, they feel unbalanced when it is not there. There is great creativity contained in 6 – a love of the arts; the voice is often used creatively. They can teach. They need to balance their lives and find harmony.

RIGHT LIKING HARMONY, LIFE PATH 6s ARE WELL-BALANCED
AND OFTEN TAKE POSITIONS OF RESPONSIBILITY,
SUCH AS THAT OF TEACHER.

Negatively, they think they know what their friends should do and tell them so. They interfere and meddle. Chauvinism (of either sex) can be present. Over-eating can be a problem. Too conventional and moralistic, they fail to see others' points of view. They worry over minor matters.

One of the creative aspects of this responsible number is shown in the Life Paths of the actresses Meryl Streep, Vanessa Redgrave and Glenda Jackson.

LIFE PATH 7: THE INDIVIDUALIST

Direction: to learn by one's own experience.
Opportunities: to use knowledge and wisdom.
Keywords: Individual. Intuitional. Deep-thinker. Analytical.
                   Mysterious. Spiritual. Perfectionist. Procrastinator.
                   Will not accept advice.

22

Sevens need to spend some time each day by themselves, for without a small amount of solitude they find it difficult to function at their best. Their talents are often specialized; they are not team people and work best alone. Achievements often occur in a surprising way and are not what was originally sought after. They have both intuitional and analytical skills but can distrust their intuition. Perfectionists, they appear to procrastinate when they are simply waiting for the perfect conditions to act. They plan secretively over a long period and then move with surprising suddenness. This Life Path is thought to dream in colour more than any other. Secretive, with deep emotions not shown willingly, they have the ability to help or heal. At heart 'a rebel', 7s are attracted to unusual or new spiritual beliefs or religions. Curiously, for a number with such spiritual potential, they can be attracted to atheism. And, surprisingly for such a solitary number, they perform well in public.

Negatively, they appear cold and arrogant, especially on first meeting. Some 7s hide from others by talking continually. They dislike physical work. They make life hard for themselves by never listening to advice. Daydreaming replaces life.

Two individual 7s, female icons of their times, are Sixties' model Jean Shrimpton, and Diana, Princess of Wales. Great political figures include President John F. Kennedy, Nikita Khrushchev, Sir Winston Churchill and Vaclav Havel.

LIFE PATH 8: THE GOAL-SETTER

Direction: to learn to set goals.
Opportunities: to become independent.
Keywords: Ambitious. Powerful. Organized. Philanthropist.
                   Dependable. Independent. Materialistic. Greedy.
                   Ruthless.

23

An enjoyment of battle and a struggle for power feature in this Life Path. Eights are strong, tough, and can be ruthless. Dynamic and independent, they dislike depending on others. They set themselves goals throughout their lives. This is a powerful and confident number working for its rewards slowly. Busy and excellent organizers, their careers are usually more important than their home lives. This is a number of extremes: success or failure. They like to look good and appearance is important. They intimidate others easily. Sporting or athletic ability is often found. When well-balanced, they are philanthropists and enjoy helping other people. This number functions well in the business world where its self-reliance and power can shine. It does not always have an easy life. It usually has to work for its success.

Negatively, they get frustrated easily. They can neglect to show affection to loved ones and are not seen at their best in domestic situations.

ABOVE THE NUMBER OF EXTREMES – SUCCESS OR FAILURE.

When greedy and over-ambitious, they start to appear unlucky.

A large roster of powerful personalities shows the self-confidence of the 8: Elizabeth Taylor, Joan Collins, Nancy Reagan, Barbra Streisand, Liza Minelli, Ginger Rogers, Jane Fonda and, amongst politicians, Saddam Hussein.

LIFE PATH 9: THE HUMANITARIAN

Direction: to learn how to show compassion.
Opportunities: to develop idealism and creativity.
Keywords: Compassionate. Humanitarian. Idealistic. Romantic. Dramatic. Creative. Magnetic. Unfocused. Temperamental.

Nine's opportunities are unlimited; this is because 9 is the only number that contains all numbers within it. Idealistic, 9s want to change the world and make life better for everyone. This is a broad-minded, tolerant and unconventional Life Path. Charismatic and creative, the dramatic power of the artist is present here. They make fine leaders of movements, cults or religions. A love of travel is present. Loving people, they prefer to deal with the large problems of life rather than the small. Dramatic endings may occur at times in their lives. They are not particularly good at financial matters, but materialism does not interest them much. Popular, other people are fascinated by their magnetic attraction. They are well suited to a life spent in the arts or humanities. Psychic ability is often present.

Negatively, they can be impatient and need to control their tempers. More practicality is needed, plus attention to detail. They are not good judges of character and may be manipulated. They can sacrifice themselves needlessly. The humanity of 9 is seen in Mahatma Gandhi; the entertainer in Shirley Maclaine and Brigitte Bardot, both in later life devoting themselves to humanitarian movements – Maclaine to the New Age, Bardot to the care of animals.

THE BIRTHCHART

CHAPTER THREE

I've had more trouble with myself than anyone else I know.
DWIGHT L. MOODY

The Life Path Number is always your most important number, but the characteristics it represents will be affected by all the numbers in your birthdate. These numbers – your birth day, your birth month and your year of birth – will strengthen or weaken the effect of your Life Path Number; this is why two people with the same Life Path can be so different. We see this effect on the Birthchart:

25

3	6	9
2	5	8
1	4	7

The Birthchart shows where each number is placed. Insert all your birthdate numbers in their appropriate squares. A zero in the date is ignored. No matter how often the same number occurs in your birthdate it should go into the same square. Someone who was

LEFT THE BIRTHCHART.

		9
2	5	8 8
1 1		

born on 1. 1. 1911, for instance, would have five 1s in the 1 square, and one 9 in the 9 square.

This is how the composer Leonard Bernstein's birth-date would appear on his Birthchart – he was born on 25 August 1918.

26

THE NEW MILLENNIUM

It is easy to see how the Birthchart can alter the effect of the Life Path Number. Here is a chart for someone born on 24. 2. 2000. He or she has a Life Path Number of 1.

This birthdate considerably softens the leadership qualities of the 1 Life Path. The Life Path number would still be the most important in the person's chart, but the three number 2s – fostering diplomatic and cooperative skills – would always have an influence.

2 2 2		
	4	

Everyone born before 2000 AD will have the number 1 on their Birthchart; everyone born in the new millennium will have a 2. These numbers represent the changing consciousness of the human race. As a generalization, babies born on or after 1. 1. 2000, and babies born on or before 31. 12. 1999, will differ fundamentally in their approach to life. The changing dates highlight the changing consciousness.

The amount of numbers in each square and the missing numbers on the chart are always considered alongside the influence of the Life Path Number. You may find the listed negative characteristics do not apply now, but earlier in life they did. Thus your Birthchart shows how you have grown and developed.

BIRTHCHART 1s

ONE 1

They express themselves easily in public, through speaking or writing. In private they need to be more open with their emotions. Strong and self-reliant. They are inclined to talk quickly.

TWO 1s

The ability to express themselves well at all times and be in control of situations in a well-balanced way. This is an effective position for work in the business or entertainment worlds.

THREE 1s

Great expressive ability, usually with the written word. Sometimes there is too much talent and the person appears hyperactive. They are usually happy people, often chatterboxes, but stubborn.

FOUR 1s AND MORE

The potential for real achievement. Frustration develops if their lives do not offer possibilities for using their powers of expression or their ability to lead. They push themselves too hard and can be careless about food and may under- or over-eat. If they allow themselves time to rest, high achievement is possible.

1 IS MISSING

This will only occur in some charts after the last day of 1999. People with the 1 missing will need to develop the qualities of self-reliance and determination. They will need to be more willing to assert themselves and not allow others to take them for granted. They will need to assert their individuality.

BIRTHCHART 2S

ONE 2

Perceptive people. They form accurate assessments of others. Sensitive, they often feel uncomfortable in a competitive environment, preferring to work at their own more peaceful pace.

TWO 2S

Awareness is heightened but they may not always heed their intuition. Sometimes mix with the wrong people. Usually their lives are well-balanced. They must beware of being overly sensitive.

THREE 2S OR MORE

Musical ability is often present. Emotional people, sensitive to others, but the need to protect their vulnerability can make them react in a cool or self-absorbed way. They can be unwilling to take action and when forced to do so, over-react.

2 IS MISSING

A need to appreciate and consider other people. Intuition and sensitivity can be distrusted. More willingness to cooperate is needed.

BIRTHCHART 3S

ONE 3

Interesting, enthusiastic and witty people. A powerful imagination that can be used in their career. Creative and bright. They help their friends when they need help. There is a strength behind this number that its bright facade does not always choose to reveal.

TWO 3S

A strong imagination which needs disciplining. There can be a dislike of practicality, a tendency to daydream and an unorthodox approach to life that may be misunderstood.

THREE 3S OR MORE

There is a strong accent on the mind and the imagination. They can daydream and neglect the present. Balancing the mind and body will benefit them. Exercise or sport may be beneficial.

3 IS MISSING

A need to be more imaginative, or a fear of, or difficulty in, expressing creativity. Mathematics is often a problem area.

BIRTHCHART 4S

ONE 4

This adds practicality. Organized, with the ability to work until the job is finished. Tenacious, loyal and dependable people. Often the craftsperson, the artisan, the painter, or the musician.

RIGHT THOSE PEOPLE WHO HAVE 4s IN THEIR BIRTHCHART ARE OFTEN PRACTICAL AND MAY BE ARTISTIC OR SHOW MUSICAL ABILITY .

TWO 4S

A need for neatness and tidiness. The ability to work long hours. They need to watch they do not become over-materialistic. Dexterity with the hands is marked.

THREE 4S OR MORE

A feeling of restriction may be felt. This is the sign of the workaholic and these people need to remember to rest. Again, wonderful ability with the hands is often present and needs to be used. They can get into a rut and find it difficult to break free.

4 IS MISSING

Practicality needs to be applied to day-to-day affairs. There can be a dislike of dealing with mundane, boring tasks. Carelessness over details causes problems and tasks may not always be finished.

BIRTHCHART 5S

ONE 5

Five is the most important number on the Birthchart. Being at the centre, it links all the other numbers. Strength and determination is marked. The 5 can motivate others. It needs freedom. There may be problems in the domestic life as it dislikes restriction.

TWO 5S

Freedom becomes important and may cause problems at home. Self-control and determination is strengthened. There is the possibility of over-confidence which can cause mistakes.

THREE 5S OR MORE

People with many 5s love to take risks in life – sometimes they get away with them. Sensuality is present although often there is an unawareness of this. Dynamic, they live life in the fast lane.

5 IS MISSING

Determination and the ability to push themselves is often absent. There is uncertainty about which direction to take and they are aware of many opportunities but do not know how to use them. They benefit from a partner who will push them into action; or a name that provides support.

BIRTHCHART 6s

ONE 6

Creative, with a desire for a peaceful domestic environment. A love of art or artistic pursuits is present. There can be creative use of the voice. They become upset if their home life is disturbed.

TWO 6s

Usually, a good memory with a fondness for food. They need to use their creativity. As with a single 6, the home will be important. Worry and anxiety is experienced over minor matters.

THREE 6s OR MORE

A more relaxed attitude to the home and family is needed. There is enormous creative potential here but it is likely that they will be distracted by domestic pressures. Anxiety is often experienced outside the home environment.

6 IS MISSING

Not particularly domesticated people. Their home life will not be the centre of

LEFT THE NUMBER 6 IN THE BIRTHCHART USUALLY EMPHASISES THE IMPORTANCE OF DOMESTICITY AND THE HOME ENVIRONMENT.

their universe. An appreciation of beauty or art may need to be developed. As children they may have been over-sensitive towards one parent. Something may be missing from their domestic life.

BIRTHCHART 7S

ONE 7

This is the most difficult number on the chart. People with this number's influence are philosophical with a need to see justice done, and dislike being taught or told what to do. This can create many hard learning experiences and life will not appear easy. Physical expression is heightened.

TWO 7S

There may be a deep interest in the meaning of life. When a 7 is on the chart, interest can develop – often late in life – in the metaphysical, spiritual or occult worlds. Life is not always easy for two 7s. They make it hard on themselves with the extreme stress they place on their individualism; they tend to dislike accepting help from others and seek their own ways of doing things.

THREE 7S OR MORE

This is sometimes seen as a sacrificial arrangement of numbers. Setbacks can be encountered. A great deal of inner knowledge is contained here, and though they make life hard for themselves – sometimes by their own actions – they philosophically accept the results and try again. They possess wisdom.

7 IS MISSING

There is often a reluctance for these people to rely upon themselves. They may fear loneliness. A distrust of anything metaphysical may be present and they tend to need proof. They are usually not over-fond of exercise.

BIRTHCHART 8S

ONE 8

Good at assessing the capabilities of others. They are excellent at organizing projects and coping with details. Tidy people. As children they can be restless. They have no problem tackling work but sometimes find difficulty in finishing it.

TWO 8S

Extremely capable people. They are shrewd in assessing others and can be intimidating. Often successful in the business world. They welcome a certain amount of change in their lives as they have unbounded mental energy that needs to be used up. There can be a distrust of the metaphysical.

THREE 8S OR MORE

A fortunate combination for a business person if they can keep a balance between the material and the spiritual. The tendency is to become materially greedy, but if this is kept in check, a well-balanced person emerges with an ability to assess others and this can be used to advantage. Often restlessness occurs.

8 IS MISSING

Organization is needed. Detailed work will be avoided and laziness or carelessness with money can be apparent. Attention to mundane tasks is needed if all that is gained is not to be lost.

BIRTHCHART 9S

ONE 9

Idealism, an awareness of the world and its people as interrelated, is shown here. During the final 100 years before 2000 AD, the 9 is on everyone's Birthchart. It signifies a subconscious awareness of the potential effects of human achievement. It has promoted a more tolerant or broad-minded attitude as the century has aged. Negatively, it has promoted aggression and war.

Two 9s

Mental activity is strong and there is dramatic and creative potential with these numbers. It is important to keep emotionalism in check. While the desire to help humanity is often felt, it is important to be aware of what is achievable in a practical sense.

		9 9
2	5	
1 1		7

Three 9s or more

These numbers show a powerful use of the intellect. A revolutionary fervour to right wrongs may be felt. These people are not good judges of character and must beware of exploitation. A charismatic and explosive combination.

LEFT JOHN F KENNEDY'S BIRTHCHART.

3		
		8 8
1 1		7

9 is missing

The dynamism of the 9 will be missing from some Birthcharts from the year 2000. Human achievements may not be so marked, but the 2 will bring cooperation. Without 9, a broader view of life needs to be developed.

LEFT EMILY BRONTE'S BIRTHCHART.

Lines on the Birthchart

A series of three numbers on your Birthchart strengthens your character in some way, depending on what the numbers are. These numbers are called Full Number Planes, Arrows of Pythagoras, or Lines. These successive numbers can be vertical: 123; 456; 789; horizontal: 369; 258; 147; or diagonal: 159; 357. It does not matter how many numbers are in each square as long as all three squares have at least one number in them. You may have more than one Line. It is possible to have five (example: born 25. 3. 1978). Three or more Birthchart Lines shows a strong personality with the possibility of easy achievement. In theory, it should be easier to gain material success and spiritual fulfilment with three or more Lines. In practice, people with no number Lines, or many numbers missing, achieve a great deal. From early in life, they are more aware of what needs to be done.

Looking at the Birthchart of President John F. Kennedy (5. 29. 1917), we see he has one complete Line: 159. This is the Line of Determination.

Three successive missing numbers on your Birthchart highlights a weakness, an area that needs to be strengthened. The Birthchart of the writer Emily Bronte (30.7.1818) shows she has one Line of missing numbers: 456. This is the Line of Frustration.

When there are two numbers on a Line, but a third number is missing, that Line is strengthened but not complete. Where two numbers on a Line are missing, it needs strengthening but is not completely weak.

Complete Number Lines

1-2-3 Line of the Planner

Good ability to make plans; to think before acting; to recognize goals and the best way to reach them. Orderly, tidy, with business expertise. Drive, cooperation and the ability to mix with others.

4-5-6 LINE OF THE WILL

Whatever they dream, whatever they want, they will concentrate on to the exclusion of everything else. Extreme will-power. Ambitions desired as a child will not willingly be given up and they hold on to a single purpose in life.

7-8-9 LINE OF ACTION

Busy, powerful, with tremendous energy. While others plan and dream they will take action. Once decisions are made they will not procrastinate. Physical energy is high but nervous headaches are associated with these characteristics. Rest, fresh air and a healthy diet are important.

3-6-9 LINE OF THE INTELLECT

Those with this Line are often logical, usually with good memories and highly intelligent. They are creative thinkers. The mind is well-balanced and problems that may come up are solved easily and quickly. They can be impatient with others who are apparently less bright.

2-5-8 LINE OF EMOTION

Love, spirituality and sensitivity towards others is usually expressed in a well-balanced way. Artistic expression driven by the emotions is often marked. There is often an ability to perform. Love is important to them and they have deep emotional needs which should be recognized and fulfilled.

1-4-7 LINE OF PHYSICALITY

Good health and physical stamina are helped with this strong line. Ability with the hands is often present (either in a practical way or artistically). Too much emphasis can be placed on the career which is oddly balanced against a revolutionary outlook. A dynamic Line that often meets set-backs in life through restrictions set up by the 4 combined with the refusal to accept help of the 7.

1-5-9 LINE OF DETERMINATION

Determined to do many things well. All babies born in the 1950s had this Line, becoming the over-achievers of the Eighties. They can persist and bounce back from set-backs. They may cling to ideas or projects when the time is long past to let go.

3-5-7 LINE OF COMPASSION

Inner calm and an acceptance of the highs and lows in life mark these people. Towards others they are understanding and compassionate. Joyful and intuitive, psychic ability is often present. Sorrows can occur, but they meet them with serene acceptance.

MISSING NUMBER LINES

1-2-3 cannot be a missing Line but when two of these numbers are missing it shows a need to think before acting, a need to plan life and its goals in a constructive way.

4-5-6 LINE OF FRUSTRATION

Sometimes called the Saturn Line. Family life can present problems. There can be a reluctance to acknowledge what is truly desired. Too much will be expected from others. They need to feel free to act without approval.

7-8-9 LINE OF INERTIA

They prefer to contemplate and perfect their ideas before acting. Procrastination may be seen by others, but this is inaccurate. They need to take action rather than merely think about it.

LEFT INNER CALM CHARACTERISES PEOPLE WITH THE 3-5-7 LINE OF COMPASSION.
THEY MAY APPEAR SERENE AND TO MEET THEIR PROBLEMS WITH ACCEPTANCE.

3-6-9 LINE OF ECCENTRICITY

Unconventional thinkers. They will not always apply logical thought to situations and may have difficulty using their creativity. They need to welcome the artistic into their lives.

2-5-8 LINE OF SENSITIVITY

Over-sensitive to the opinions of others. As children there can be a lack of self-confidence, an inferiority complex. Introverted and not usually comfortable in large groups, they need to like themselves more.

1-4-7 LINE OF ILLUSION

Practical matters and materialism will be of little concern. A need to take more dynamic action in life. Physical stamina may be weak and they may dislike being alone. Life can be lived in a rut and a less conforming spirit will need to be developed.

38

1-5-9 LINE OF RESIGNATION

Originality, motivation and determination may be lacking. When containing full numbers this Line is exciting and strengthening; when missing, a lack of purpose and a feeling of resignation prevails. They need to beware of always following others.

3-5-7 LINE OF THE SCEPTIC

This Line has two meanings. The first is for people who demand proof, are suspicious of anything metaphysical (such as this book) and orthodox in their beliefs. The second meaning appears more frequently today: open-minded, welcoming new ideas and beliefs – the opposite of the first. A Line that appears to offer a choice. Migraines and nervous complaints are associated with it.

RIGHT THOSE WITH THE 3-5-7 LINE OF THE SCEPTIC ARE OFTEN SUSPICIOUS OF BELIEFS THAT ARE NOT ORTHODOX AND OBVIOUSLY PROVEN.

THE BIRTHDAY AND GOAL NUMBERS

CHAPTER FOUR

All things which can be known have number,
for it is not possible that without number anything
can be either conceived or known.

PHILOLAUS

Your Birthday Number is the number of your day of birth. It represents how you think and act when you are alone and how you interact in everyday situations. It influences your Life Path but is not as important. It does not represent your direction in life, or opportunities or show your main talents. There should be no difficulty recognizing yourself and your actions from this number. Friends may recognize you from your Birthday Number more easily than they do from your Life Path. It is your second lucky number – second in strength to the Life Path, this time regarding good fortune.

The following brief description of your birthday is added to the information obtained from your Life Path and Birthchart. Birthdays number 1 – 31 are listed. Negative and positive aspects are included, the positive being stronger.

BIRTHDAYS

1ST Leadership and ego. A dislike of taking orders from other people. Self-employment attracts, or any original line of work. A need to stand alone. Determined, courageous and self-confident. There can be a disinclination to show affection. People born this day: Boris Yeltsin, J.D. Salinger.

2ND Cooperative and hesitant. Loving, sensitive and intuitive. Can work with or for others. Likes partnership or teamwork. Kindness is a positive trait. Easily becomes discouraged or depressed. Born this day: Mahatma Gandhi, Dr Benjamin Spock.

3RD Happy and jealous. Gregarious, popular and sociable. Brings laughter and joy to any group. A natural wit. Often a hidden fear of loneliness. Can be restless. Fun to be with but easily bored. Born this day: Gore Vidal, Gertrude Stein.

4TH Stable but gets into a rut. A practical hard worker. Stability is important. A need to build the life on secure foundations. A loyal, patient and honest friend. Attracted to the orthodox and often uncomfortable with change, preferring order. A good day for politicians and doctors. Born this day: Dr Thomas Barnardo, Francisco Franco.

5TH Adventurous and self-indulgent. Enthusiastic and versatile. Forever seeking the 'new'. Progressive with an unconscious sexuality. A love of travel and change. A surprisingly good birthdate for politicians. Born this day: William S. Burroughs, Raquel Welch

6TH Responsible and anxious. Many teachers are born on this day. Concerned with justice. They make reliable friends. Creative people with a need to live in harmony. A strong love for their family about whom they worry unnecessarily. Born this day: Sigmund Freud, Elizabeth Barrett Browning.

7TH Individualistic but procrastinating. Silent and secretive. Needs solitude to stay well-balanced. Analytical and intuitive, often absorbed in thought and attracted to the spiritual or occult. Born this day: Saint Bernadette, Billy Graham.

8TH Goal-setting and greedy. Seeking independence. Good organizational ability. Many writers and scientists are born on this day. A balance needed between the career and the home – usually the career dominates. Born this day: Katharine Hepburn, Dr Christiaan Barnard.

9TH Compassionate and quick-tempered. A love for humanity. Broadminded. Emotional and dramatic. Creative and idealistic with serious aims. Practicality often needed. Born this day: Simone de Beauvoir, Glenda Jackson.

10TH Original and self-centred. Similar to the 1st. Self-confident and self-assured. Many actors born under this number. Single minded. Great energy. Arrogance needs to be watched. Born this day: Fred Astaire, Marcel Proust.

11TH Inspired and impractical. Similar to the 2nd. Ability to cooperate. Not over-concerned about financial matters. Music and rhythm attracts. Daydreaming has to be curbed. Leadership ability preferably with help from a strong partner. A charismatic day. Many artists born here. Born this day: Irving Berlin, Martha Graham.

12TH Creative but sacrificial. Similar to the 3rd. Bringing many singers and musicians into the world. Popular and gregarious with the ability to get things done. There are often ups and downs in life. Periods of sacrifice but always with the ability to cope. Born this day: Frank Sinatra, Maria Callas.

13TH Achieving and self-destructive. Similar to the 4th. A practical number with the ability to create change on a large scale. Hard working. Needing to listen more to the opinions of others. More vulnerable and emotional than they appear. Born this day: Fidel Castro, Arnold Schoenberg.

14TH Analytical but pleasure-seeking. Similar to the 5th. Full of curiosity, with a sybaritic approach to life. Often can be attractive and sensual people – attracting many hangers-on. When self-disciplined much can be accomplished. Travel attracts. Born this day: Cecil Beaton, Albert Einstein.

15TH Just but meddlesome. Similar to the 6th. Responsible with a love of fair play. Home life is important but they dislike spending all their time there. Original people with a love of beauty. Vanity has to be watched. They learn new ways easily. Born this day: Florence Nightingale, Martin Luther King.

16TH Intuitive and nervous. Similar to the 7th. Needing solitude. Self-critical, setting themselves high standards. A dislike of interference in their affairs. Religion, medicine and writing are careers this number is often attracted to. They need to relax. Born this day: Noel Coward, Oscar Wilde.

17TH Physical and reckless. Similar to the 8th. Traditionally considered a good number for financial matters, although life is often success or failure for 17. There is usually physical ability. Sportspeople and dancers are often born under this number. Born this day: Rudolf Nureyev, Rita Hayworth.

18TH Powerful but materialistic. Similar to the 9th. Broad-minded with wide-ranging interests. Friction may be felt between acting for the good of others and putting themselves first. Leadership is often given to them – even when they do not seek it. Born this day: Greta Garbo, Lucrezia Borgia.

19TH Independent but arrogant. Similar to the 1st. They tackle life in an original way and dislike receiving advice but always consider the needs of others. Moods can be up one minute, down the next. Emotional people. Born this day: Coco Chanel, Jean Genet.

20TH Kind but anxious. Similar to the 2nd. Loving people. They dislike taking action without the approval of others. Good at detailed work. Musical and artistic. They easily become pessimistic. Born this day: Sergei Rachmaninov, Henrik Ibsen.

21ST Lucky but extravagant. Similar to the 3rd. Considered a 'lucky' number. Attractive and cheerful, often in the right place at the right time, and the centre of attention. A need to concentrate so opportunities are not lost. Born this day: Florenz Ziegfeld, Robin Williams.

22ND Masterful and dominating. Similar to the 4th. Considered the most powerful day to be born on. Natural leaders. Nervous tension needs watching. They rarely doubt their instincts which are usually accurate. Born this day: Mrs Rose Kennedy, D.W. Griffith.

23RD Freedom-seeking but over-indulgent. Similar to the 5th. Loving change, freedom and pleasure. This number can hesitate to express its real emotions. Anything new appeals. An interesting, if untameable, personality. Born this day: Joan Crawford, Joan Collins.

24TH Artistic and over-serious. Similar to the 6th. The decorative arts attract. The home is an important place. Trustworthy, loyal and friendly. Born this day: Henri de Toulouse-Lautrec, Barbra Streisand.

25TH A perfectionist but secretive. Similar to the 7th. Freedom seeking, making decisions slowly. Calm, with insight. Can appear shy at first. Able to keep secrets. Born this day: Pablo Picasso, Virginia Woolf.

26TH Charismatic but over-stressed. Similar to the 8th. Dependable and well-organized. Revolutionary thinkers with financial ability and, surprisingly, a love of domesticity. A balance is kept between home and career. If in business they often have artistic hobbies. Born this day: Mao Tse-tung, Leon Trotsky.

27TH Humanitarian but impatient. Similar to the 9th. Independent thinking with a calm manner. Hard to anger but intimidating when aroused. Religion or science often attracts. Travel is often enjoyed. There is usually a vivid imagination. Born this day: Confucius, Mother Teresa of Calcutta.

28TH Initiative shown but selfish. Similar to the 1st. Self-employment or leadership attracts, although this number succeeds best with a partner. A combination of determination, originality and perception. A strong will with the ability to mix with others. Born this day: Jacqueline Onassis, Beatrix Potter.

44

29TH Protective but scattered. Similar to the 2nd. A sparkling, musical, inspiring personality. An emotional and dramatic life at times. They need to comfort others. Spiritual, with strong beliefs, sometimes allowing themselves to be manipulated. Born this day: Oprah Winfrey, Michael Jackson.

30TH Entertaining and easily bored. Similar to the 3rd. Has many friends and is the centre of attention. A love of life is usually present. They possess a wit that is too insightful at times. Often happy people who scatter their energy around them. Born this day: Truman Capote, Sir Winston Churchill.

31ST Attractive but orthodox. Similar to the 4th. Potent mix of practical and creative. Combination of hard worker and artist. Unselfish, with distinctive good taste. Intuition and practicality combined can cause stress. Born this day: Anna Pavlova, Norman Mailer.

THE BIRTHDAY NUMBER

In conventional numerology, fadic addition is used on your Birthday Number, as this shows its true essence. If there are two digits in your number (as in 11, 23) add them together, continuing until a single digit is left. This is the same process we applied to find the Life Path Number.

From now on, when your Birthday Number is mentioned, it will be the fadic number that is referred to. The general traits of each Birthday Number are:

1 (or 10, 19 & 28) Leading. Original. Self-confident.

2 (or 11, 20 & 29) Cooperative. Friendly. Kind.

3 (or 12, 21 & 30) Creative. Self-expressive. Witty.

4 (or 13, 22 & 31) Practical. Self-disciplined. Hard working.

5 (or 14 & 23) Communicative. Freedom-seeking. Versatile.

6 (or 15 & 24) Responsible. Creative. Advisory.

7 (or 16 & 25) Intuitive. Analytical. Solitary.

8 (or 17 & 26) Ambitious. Goal-setting. Independent.

9 (or 18 & 27) Compassionate. Dramatic. Idealistic.

Sometimes, it is easier to use your Birthday characteristics than those of your Life Path. If the two numbers are the same number there is no problem; but if different, your Life Path always shows your true direction – your path to fulfilment. Following the Birthday and ignoring the Life Path will lead to frustration.

The Birthday adds talents and strengths to the Life Path. As the Life Path is always the most important, what you receive from your Birthday Number may help or hinder your Life Path talents.

If your Life Path and Birthday are different numbers, but both odd or both even, the combination is harmonious. You will be aware of the two sides of your personality but will not experience many inner problems. For instance: the actor Robert Redford has a 1 Life Path, and a 9 Birthday. His important trait would be that of the leader, the initiator, but he would also have the humanitarian qualities of the 9. Likewise, someone with the vitality of a 5 Life Path would be a calmer person with the effect of a 7 Birthday Number.

If you have one even and one odd number, there is a certain amount of conflict. The important point to remember is that the Life Path is the track to follow in life. If the qualities of the Life Path are consciously cultivated, problems in life gradually ease.

THE GOAL NUMBER

There is another important number in your birthdate: the Goal Number. It represents what you can achieve – what your Life Path is leading you to. It is third in importance. Disregarding this 'goal' usually brings out the negative tendencies of the number. It is found by adding your Birthday Number and month of birth together, using fadic addition to reduce to a single digit.

For instance: Jacqueline Onassis was born on the 28th July – adding 28 (Birthday 1) and 7 (July) together, we get her Goal Number, which is 8.

Goal Number 1: The goal is leadership.

Goal Number 2: The goal is friendship.

Goal Number 3: The goal is to express creativity.

Goal Number 4: The goal is practical achievement.

Goal Number 5: The goal is freedom.

Goal Number 6: The goal is accepting responsibility.

Goal Number 7: The goal is wisdom and self-knowledge.

Goal Number 8: The goal is material success.

Goal Number 9: The goal is expressing universal love.

LEFT GOAL NUMBER 2: THE GOAL IS FRIENDSHIP.

THE VOWEL NUMBER

CHAPTER FIVE

A name is a kind of face.
THOMAS FULLER

Your name affects what you want, how other people see you, and most importantly what you do. To say that a name has any effect appears to some a foolish statement. But if a word and its sounds can affect us – and all words do – this must also apply to your name.

Think how long parents spend selecting the right name for their child. A baby recognizes this name at between one and two years old,

---

THE IMPORTANCE OF NAMES

In a book on the Hebrew system of numerology, *Numera*, the writer Bernard Spencer Le Gette offers an original illustration of how names affect us. He suggests that we imagine everyone was called by the first line of a song – instead of a name. Imagine if every day you were called by and responded to the line from the carol: 'Silent night, holy night'; or how would you react or become a different person if your name was, 'You're simply the best!'?

its last name around the age of three. This name becomes a personal symbol. It feels inseparable from you and you hear it day after day. Your name is not as inseparable from you as your birthdate. It may feel so but it is not, it has been chosen by you or your parents. It can always be changed – your birthdate cannot.

The name you are known by is your *real* name. This name contains the sounds that affect you day in, day out. This name gives an accurate analysis. Your full birth certificate name is what you started life with. The name you are now called is what you have become.

ABOVE A BABY RECOGNIZES ITS NAME AT BETWEEN ONE AND TWO YEARS OLD AND THIS NAME BECOMES AN IMPORTANT PERSONAL SYMBOL.

If your name is hyphenated like Mary-Jane, or spoken as one, as in Billy Ray, analyse this as one name, as long as Mary-Jane and not Mary is the name you are called. Include middle names and initials only if you always use them.

Your name is affected by the numbers of your Life Path and Birthday and the pattern on your Birthchart. If the Birthchart pattern is strong – three or more Lines – the name will have slightly less effect than if the Birthchart is weak. A good name, one that compliments your Life Path, is an advantage and to be desired.

Your first name affects your personal affairs and has a strong influence on you when you are alone; your last name or surname usually represents family or inherited traits and, unless you are always addressed by it, will have less influence.

Your full name – first and last names (and for some people middle name as well) combined – influences your public persona and represents the 'total' you. This full or complete name contains your most important name numbers and the table below shows the letters of the alphabet and the numbers that correspond to them. A is 1 and Z is 26. Fadic addition is used on all the letters of the alphabet that have double numbers: from 10 to 26 – from J to Z. Using this we see that A(1), J(10), and S(19) are all represented by the number 1. This means that A, J and S are all related.

1	2	3	4	5	6	7	8	9
A	B	C	D	E	F	G	H	I
J	K	L	M	N	O	P	Q	R
S	T	U	V	W	X	Y	Z	

The vowels show what motivates you. The consonants affect how you see yourself when alone and the first impression your personality makes on others. The total number obtained from the vowels and consonants combined shows how you interact with other people.

The vowel number has many names: Motivation, Soul Urge, Ambition, Heart's Desire, and others. We will simply call it the Vowel Number. It shows what is wanted from life, what is desired. The vowel sounds are the inner life of the name, hence they show the inner or hidden motivation.

The vowels are A, E, I, O and U. Some numerologists also use Y, some never, and some only if there is no other vowel in the name. It is suggested you use Y as a vowel only if there is no other vowel in the same syllable: in Sally, Y would be a vowel; in Rodney, Y would not be a vowel. If you have Y in your name, try calculating it both as a vowel and again as a consonant. You will recognize which way is right for you. The influence of Y means you can be motivated in two different ways.

THE VOWEL NUMBER

Using the table on p.48, we place the numbers for each vowel above the letter in the name. We then continue to add all the numbers together (fadic addition) until one single number is left and the final total is the Vowel Number. Here is the Vowel Number for the name of the tennis player Andre Agassi:

1			5		1		1		9	= 17, 1 + 7 =	Vowel Number 8
A	N	D	R	E		A	G	A	S	S I	

THE VOWEL NUMBERS

VOWEL NUMBER 1

Wanting to take the lead; they like to see their ideas and wishes promoted. They prefer to work alone and can enjoy self-employment. An original and unorthodox path is preferred. They seek independence. Usually optimistic with a sense of humour. They may disregard the wishes of others – they want their own way. Once they make a decision they will be impatient to begin.

VOWEL NUMBER 2

Wanting to cooperate and work easily with others. They may be reticent or shy about making the first move and sometimes prefer someone else to take the first step. They dislike being rushed and prefer life at a slow and steady pace. Uncomfortable in a highly competitive environment. Attracted to music and rhythm. They wish to be inspired.

VOWEL NUMBER 3

Wanting to have fun. They desire pleasant conditions and a lively atmosphere. Ambitious with a need to use creativity in whatever they do. When work is finished they want to party and enjoy themselves. Great talkers, they like having people around and need constant stimulation otherwise they get bored. Threes are attracted to the glamour of life. Good at judging others' motives. At times they can be vain and jealous.

VOWEL NUMBER 4

Wanting an orderly and organized life. Practical, distrusting the unconventional. Stability and security are important. They are not afraid of hard work but can feel restricted and become stuck-in-a-rut. If they feel dull for a long time they dramatically alter their desires, but most of the time they abhor sudden change. Fours feel comfortable with set boundaries.

VOWEL NUMBER 5

Wanting freedom and an unrestricted lifestyle. They need to communicate with others and are always interested in new ideas. Versatile and adapting instantly to changing circumstances. They change their interests when they have experienced something completely. Travel always appeals. Sex is usually important. Restless, they can over-indulge themselves in pleasure.

VOWEL NUMBER 6

Wanting to help and easily accepting responsibility. They need to see justice done and have a strong sense of right and wrong. They wish to see others behave as responsibly as themselves, need a quiet and harmonious home life and desire and want to give love. Creative ability needs to be used. Perfection seekers.

VOWEL NUMBER 7

Wanting time alone to think. They need to make up their own minds. They analyse everything but also use intuition. Strong sense of their own individuality and like to keep their secrets to themselves. They have a love of nature – often the sea. If unable to spend time alone with their thoughts they feel unbalanced.

VOWEL NUMBER 8

Wanting to achieve their goals. Ambitious with a powerful urge to succeed. They strive for independence. Logical and organized in their aims, they can take ruthless decisions. They have powerful desires and experience frustration and bafflement if they do not fulfil them. Tend to blame themselves. They need to relax more. If personal needs are gratified they will then help others who are less fortunate.

51

VOWEL NUMBER 9

Wanting to see their ideals played out in life. They are understanding and feel compassion for others. They like to travel. A wide range of interests. Unfortunately, they can scatter their energy over too many projects. Romantic and life is experienced on a grand scale. They have creative desires they need to satisfy. Too trusting of others, they have a strong love of life.

The effect your Vowel Number has on you depends on the number of your Life Path. Should both numbers (Vowel and Life Path) be the same, there will be no conflict in what you want out of life. This is the best combination to have.

If the numbers are different there will be some conflict. If both numbers are odd, or both even, this is not seriously conflicting – the numbers are complimentary and support each other.

If one number is odd and the other even, there is conflict. Your Life Path will be bringing you opportunities that you do not want. The Vowel Number will create dreams and desires that are incompatible with your abilities and talents. When we

ABOVE TRAVEL IS IMPORTANT TO VOWEL NUMBER 9 AND THEY LOVE LIFE. HOWEVER, THEY CAN SPREAD THEIR ENERGIES TOO WIDELY.

later look at the complete name number you may find you act more in keeping with your Life Path. The Life Path always shows the right direction to guide your actions.

If your Vowel Number is the same as your Birthday Number, care should be taken not to place too much emphasis on your Birthday characteristics at the expense of your Life Path (this only applies to Birthdays and Life Paths that are different).

THE CONSONANT NUMBER

CHAPTER SIX

It is only shallow people who do not judge by appearances.

OSCAR WILDE

The consonants in your name, added together, show the image you project to strangers. This consonant number may not represent what you want, nor how you ultimately act but it shows how you present yourself to others; it influences how you see yourself when you are alone. It is closer to the influence of the Birthday than the Life Path.

This number has many names: the Personality, the Inner Self, the Impression, the Latent or Quiescent Self and others. We will call it the Consonant Number. To find it we use the alphabet table (*see* p.48). Place the appropriate number beneath each consonant in your name. Use fadic addition to reduce to a single digit. Here is an example:

W I N S T O N   C H U R C H I L L
5   5 1 2   5   3 8   9 3 8   3 3   = 55, 5 + 5 = 10, 1 + 0 = 1
Winston Churchill has a Consonant Number of 1.

ELIZABETH TAYLOR

**The first impression given by the Consonant Number can differ
from the motivation shown by the Vowel Number. For example:**

```
5  9  1  5        1    6      = 27, 2 + 7 = 9
E  L  I  Z  A  B  E  T  H     T  A  Y  L  O  R
  3  8  2  2 8     2  7 3    9   = 44, 4 + 4 = 8
```

**Elizabeth Taylor's Consonant Number (8) gives a powerful, worldly
and ambitious image; the Vowel Number (9) shows the motivation
of the humanitarian. The projected image is more ambitious than
what is desired. Here, Y has been used as a consonant, but Y as a
vowel would still show a difference between the numbers.**

THE CONSONANT NUMBERS

CONSONANT NUMBER 1

The image is that of the leader. Number 1s stride on to the stage of life
with initiative, determination and originality. Happy, often instantly
popular, there is an air of self-reliance and self-confidence about
them, even if they do not feel it. They sometimes make enemies with
their enthusiasm to see their own plans followed through. They
appear to be unlikely to work well in a team situation.

CONSONANT NUMBER 2

The image is that of the friendly cooperator. They cope well when
diplomatic skills are needed. Tact and the ability to provide advice,
comfort and help are displayed. Inspirational, but always in a quiet
way. There can be a degree of shyness at first and they will not always
make the first move. They are seen as easy-going and natural people
who make good friends. Negatively, they can appear sly.

CONSONANT NUMBER 3

The image is of a bright, witty and happy person. Creativity is marked. There is a love of life, an enthusiasm for having a good time. Gregarious people who come alive at social events, they appear restless and easily bored. The image is of someone who possesses abundant good luck.

CONSONANT NUMBER 4

The image is of a person with organizational skills who acts in a practical way in a crisis. A hard worker who is emotionally stable and self-contained. Appearing self-disciplined, good at detailed work, they easily handle boring everyday chores. An orthodox and conservative personality. They prefer the natural to the artificial, appearing predictable but solid.

CONSONANT NUMBER 5

The image is one of versatility. They appear to have many talents, to be able to turn their hands to almost anything. Quick reactions.

SADDAM HUSSEIN

A word spelt differently in another language (but using the same common alphabet, such as French or Italian) will show through its numbers the differing approaches of each culture. Names should be analysed using their own alphabet. The following name is not an accurate analysis as the original name is not written in English, but see how the Vowel and Consonant Numbers affect our perception:

```
  1       1        3     5 9    = 19, 1 + 9 = 10, 1 + 0 = 1
  S A D D A M    H U S S E I N
  1   4 4   4      8   1 1    5  = 28, 2 + 8 = 10, 1 + 0 = 1
```

Insightful and enthusiastic. They appear progressive and want to try anything new. Hard to pin down and forever seeking freedom. There is a sexual attractiveness often displayed on first meeting and they appear more promiscuous than they are. Others are never quite sure about them. A dazzling paradox.

CONSONANT NUMBER 6

The image is one of creativity allied with a sense of responsibility. They appear harmonious and well-balanced. There is also a love of beauty. They appear to work well as part of a team, or would make a responsible partner. May be attracted to teaching. The home environment seems to be their place of happiness. Over-anxious at times. A doting parent.

CONSONANT NUMBER 7

The image is one of coolness, independence and deep thinking. They are hard to get to know at first. Solitary and secretive, they give nothing away. Individualistic, they will not accept advice and insist on going their own way. They appear arrogant although this is just natural reserve. They are not afraid to make the first move, they just do not want to.

CONSONANT NUMBER 8

The image is strong, self-assured and capable. Appearing ambitious and determined to make a success of their lives. Goal-oriented, their lives do not always appear easy. There can be an undercurrent of struggle or ill luck. The extremes of success or failure can typify 8. Tenacious survivors who are kind to others. Sometimes greedy and materialistic, they need to feel in control.

RIGHT THE IMAGE OF CONSONANT NUMBER 8 IS OF STRENGTH AND SELF-ASSUREDNESS. THEY LIKE TO FEEL IN CONTROL.

CONSONANT NUMBER 9

The image is dramatic, romantic and idealistic. A love of people and a broad-minded approach to life. There is a charismatic quality to this number. They appear compassionate humanitarians with an unconventional approach. Independent and creative. A dynamic presence that attracts others to them. Energetic, with a quick, exploding bad temper. Life appears far from dull.

The Consonant Number is not as important as the Vowel Number. What you want from life will always have a stronger influence on you than how you may appear. Nevertheless, it is still an important number and you will need to judge its effect with your Life Path. If it is the same as your Life Path, the first impression you give is likely to be how you really are. But this may not show what you ultimately do, nor what you desire.

   If your Consonant Number and Life Path are both odd or both even numbers, it is a harmonious combination. If one number is odd and the other even, the impression you give is different from your true self. You may appear to others as an unlikely candidate for the opportunities that come your way.

STRESS NUMBERS

To find any Stress Number you subtract one number from the other. It can be used to show the main problems between your Life Path and Vowel, your Vowel and Consonant, or any two numbers. Two even or two odd numbers subtracted from each other will not manifest conflicts as easily as when one number is odd and the other even.

RIGHT STRESS NUMBER 3. LIFE MAY BE TAKEN TOO SERIOUSLY, WITH AN OVER-EMPHASIS ON WORKING AND ROUTINE. AN INABILITY TO BE SOCIABLE AND ENJOY LIFE MAY BE PRESENT.

As an example: Jane Austen's Consonant Number was 5, her Life Path was 3 (numbers suggesting communication, curiosity and creativity). Her Stress Number here was 2 (5 − 3 = 2). Although Life Path and Consonant are both odd − suggesting a harmonious combination − her Stress Number shows if problems arose it would have been over cooperating, sharing, being willing to follow, and so on. All qualities of 2.

Movie star Greta Garbo's Life Path was 6, and her Consonant Number 9 (a combination of creativity). Her Stress Number here was 3. The three shows a difficulty with her image of projecting fun, laughter and gregariousness. She may even at times have been unwilling to use her creativity. It highlights her famous statement: 'I want to be alone.'

The positive and negative characteristics of the two numbers used to find the Stress Number are always more important. The Stress Number provides additional information.

MEANING OF STRESS NUMBERS

0 NO STRESS NUMBER
This only occurs when both numbers are of the same value. A zero denotes little stress. Any difficulties that arise will be found in the negative aspects of the number involved.

1 Stress is shown over-taking the initiative, taking the lead, being willing to forge ahead in an original way. There can be hesitancy to start anything new. A lack of ambition or dependency on others. Courage is sometimes lacking.

2 Stress is shown over being able to cooperate with others. There can be inability to show sensitivity or a dislike of displaying affection. A tendency to be unable to follow directions. There may be a dislike of sharing. A peaceful atmosphere can be difficult to maintain.

3 Stress is shown by taking life too seriously. Self-expression is difficult. Discomfort is felt in crowds, an inability to socialize. Enjoyment and pleasure are problem areas. A refusal sometimes to use creative talents.

4 Stress is shown over the need to consider the practical side of life. A refusal to lay down constructive plans for the future. A dislike of hard work or repetitive tasks is a problem. There is a lack of patience or tenacity.

5 Stress is shown over adaptability. An unwillingness to accept change or try anything new. There is a fear of freedom. A preference for staying put. Sexual needs may be ignored. An unwillingness to mix with others is felt. Competition is disliked.

6 Stress is shown related to the home. A dislike of accepting responsibility. Domestic life is a problem area. Creative pursuits may be cast aside. There is a lack of balance. Life feels uneven. It is difficult not to become over-anxious.

59

7 Stress is shown when left alone; a fear of loneliness or a dislike of working by oneself. There is a fear of psychoanalysis, a dislike of probing inner motives. Learning by personal experience is avoided.

8 Stress is shown over career issues or matters of independence. Organizational skills can be lacking. Self-confidence is weak. A feeling of confusion. Showing ambition is deemed unhealthy and there is an inability to choose a definite goal in life.

THE NAME AND POWER NUMBERS

CHAPTER SEVEN

Names and natures do often agree.
JOHN CLARKE

Numerologists use many different names for the number of the name: Expression, Destiny, Character and others. For simplicity, we will call it the Name Number. It represents the complete name you are known by (first – sometimes middle – and last names combined). The total of all your letters. It is the most important number you have control of. You have power or control over it because you can change it. Many people do this unconsciously when they respond to a nickname. Women in Western society often do this on marriage.

The Name Number represents what you do – it shows how you interact with other people. In this sense it has an effect on the situations you attract, but this influence is small compared to the opportunities the Life Path brings.

Numerologically, having the right name is important. There is an ancient belief that words that total the same number are connected. For instance: God, majestic, eminent, grand, zeal, smart, mega, success, influence and renown, all total the number 8. Words with the same number as your Name Number are related in some way.

NAME NUMBER

Your Name Number is the fadic total of all the numbers in your name when added together; or the total of your Vowel and Consonant Numbers combined. It is the same thing. Here is how to calculate it:

6	6		1	5	= 18, 1 + 8 = 9	Vowel: 9
C O C O		C H A N E L				Consonant: 7
3	3	3 8	5	3	= 25, 2 + 5 = 7	16, 1 + 6 = 7 Name

THE NAME NUMBERS

NAME NUMBER 1

They interact with others in an original and assertive way. They easily take the lead and are not afraid of striding ahead into new fields alone. They prefer to take charge.

Negatively

They experience difficulty in following orders. May act in a too-determined manner and can be impatient.

Examples

Winston Churchill and Mahatma Gandhi.

NAME NUMBER 2

They interact with others in a friendly, diplomatic and cooperative manner. They attract and inspire people. There is an artistic need. They cope well with details and patiently wait until the time is right to act. They dislike being rushed.

Negatively

They may be indecisive and duplicitous.

Examples

Martin Luther King and Ronald Reagan.

NAME NUMBER 3

They interact with others in a vital and lively manner. They express themselves well and often use wit and laughter to further their aims. Gregarious, they look for social interaction. There is a need to use their creativity.

Negatively

They may get bored and have difficulty finishing what is started.

Examples

Maggie Smith and Lauren Bacall.

NAME NUMBER 4

They interact with others in a stable and unemotional manner. They follow a practical and logical approach, making certain before acting that their plans will work. Orthodox, they tend to push themselves too hard, becoming workaholics.

Negatively

They may get into a rut, becoming dull and rigid in their thinking.

Examples

Margaret Thatcher and Greta Garbo.

NAME NUMBER 5

Adaptable and versatile when interacting with others. They prefer to take a new or different approach to life. Disliking restrictions they will seek an element of freedom. They communicate well, having the ability to motivate others, and are usually popular.

Negatively

They may change direction too often or get lost in pleasure seeking.

Examples

Elvis Presley and Liza Minelli.

Name Number 6

Loving and harmonious when interacting with others. Unafraid of responsibility and will offer a helping hand. A peaceful home life is needed for them to function at their best. They need to use their creativity.

Negatively

They may tell others what to do and interfere needlessly.

Examples

Brigitte Bardot and Bruce Springsteen.

Name Number 7

Individualistic when interacting with others. The easy or accepted way to do something is ignored. They need to prove to themselves that things work. Time alone to think is needed. A dislike of being taught.

Negatively

They may daydream and defer taking action until conditions are perfect – which may be too late.

Examples

Michael Jackson and Arnold Schwarzenegger.

Name Number 8

They interact with others by setting goals to achieve. Efficient and capable with a businesslike approach. Ambitious whether they want success or not.

Negatively

They may become greedy and power hungry.

Examples

Elizabeth Taylor and Warren Beatty.

Name Number 9

Broad-minded, tolerant, compassionate when interacting with others. They need to use their creativity. Their approach is idealistic. There is a liking for travel and a need for a wide panorama on which to act.

Negatively

They may be impractical and spend all their money.

Examples

Judy Garland and James Dean.

Your Life Path and Name Number are important areas of your chart. If both numbers are the same there is little stress between what you do and the opportunities you attract. It is a fortunate combination to have. If both numbers are odd, or both even, it is still harmonious, although not perfect. One number odd and the other even is a difficult combination. You may not always take full advantage of the opportunities that come your way.

RIGHT A NEGATIVE ASPECT TO NAME NUMBER 9 IS A TENDENCY TO BE IMPRACTICAL AND TO BE PROFLIGATE WITH MONEY.

POWER NUMBERS

Add your Life Path to your Name Number (using fadic addition) and you discover your Number of Power. It has a subtle effect on your chart and reveals what can be attained from the combined effect of your Life Path and Name.

As an example: Margaret Roberts had a 4 Life Path and a 9 Name Number, giving her a 4 Power Number. The hardworking aspect of her Life Path was combined with the idealism of the 9 Name. The Power 4 would have helped her towards constructive achievements, although a 5 Stress Number would have indicated difficulties with freedom, communication, and a distrust of anything new.

When Margaret Roberts married and became Margaret Thatcher her Name Number changed to 4. Her Life Path and Name were now the same. There was little stress between what she would do and her natural talents. An excellent combination. Her Power Number became 8, the natural number of the powerful tycoon or executive. This does not mean she would have been unable to have become a powerful political figure as Margaret Roberts, but the change of name to Thatcher would have made the difficult climb up the political greasy pole easier.

POWER NUMBERS

The Power Number shows the easiest position attained from the combined effect of your Name Number and Life Path. Here is how to find it: the painter Pablo Picasso's Life Path was 8; his Name Number was 2: 8 + 2 = 10, 1 + 0 = 1. The Power Number was 1. Picasso had a strong but not easy Life Path, plus a 2 Name. The 2 would influence seeking a partner and foster artistic expression. His Power Number, a 1, helped achieve a position of originality.

MEANING OF POWER NUMBERS

1 Life is influenced by original thinking and methods, determination to achieve, and a brave and courageous ambition. The achievement is that of the pioneering leader, the originator of new ideas, the inventor of new things.

2 Life is influenced by the ability to work well with others, to collaborate, to use tact and diplomacy. The achievement is that of the inspired artist, the true friend, the peacemaker.

3 Life is influenced by using self-expression, bringing happiness, joy and laughter to others. The achievement is that of the creator, the entertainer, the joy-bringer.

4 Life is influenced by an ability to create a stable environment, being able to take a practical approach, laying strong foundations. The achievement is attained after steady progress: the constructive builder, the reliable person.

5 Life is influenced by communication, being at ease with others, seeking freedom and progress. The achievement is popularity with others, the person with many and varying interests, the natural talker and salesperson.

6 Life is influenced by taking responsibility, using creativity and bringing harmony to others. The achievement is that of the teacher, the artist, the protector.

7 Life is influenced by an ability to use solitude constructively, to use intuition and seek inner growth. The achievement is an awareness of spirituality and its values, a philosophical outlook, a consciousness of individuality.

8 Life is influenced by projecting power, being efficient and working slowly towards material rewards. The achievement is that of the business executive, the philanthropist, the achiever of material wealth and rewards.

9 Life is influenced by the ability to understand others, to be broad-minded, to place a high value on showing compassion. The achievement is that of the dramatic artist, unlimited fulfilment and seeking independence.

THE FIRST NAME NUMBER

You may want to analyse each of your names individually. This is advisable. Your complete name – as in your Name Number – is still your most important number, followed by your Vowel and Consonant Numbers. But your first name, in particular, has a definite effect on your personal life.

The First Name Number is sometimes called the Key, or the Core. It is found by adding, fadically, all the numbers in the first name together. It is affected by your Birthday Number. Whatever your Birthday Number is, it is better to have a First Name Number that is different, otherwise your Birthday characteristics risk being strengthened instead of those of your Life Path.

If your Life Path and Birthday are the same number, it is still better to have a different First Name Number. Traditionally, the first name is the 'key' to open the door to life; if the Birthday, the 'lock', is the same, you will not be able to open the door yourself and will need the assistance of others.

Numbers are traditionally associated with the four elements. It is thought better, by some numerologists, not to have the Birthday and First Name from the same number group. The groups are:

THE FOUR ELEMENTS

Fire: 1 3 9   Air: 5 6   Earth: 4 6 8   Water: 2 7

The number 6 can be in two groups. For characteristics of your First Name, consult the Name Numbers in this chapter. The Vowel and Consonant Numbers of your First Name can be analysed in the same way as for your complete name but applied on a more private or personal level.

Your last name usually shows inherited influences of your family. For most people nowadays their first name will be more important.

THE ALPHABET

I often think how much easier life would have been for me and how much time I should have saved if I had known the alphabet.

W. SOMERSET MAUGHAM

The first letter of a word dominates the letters that follow it. It is often called the Cornerstone. It shows you your materialistic attitude and your thinking reaction to the world around you. It is not always listened to or acted upon but it has a subtle effect on your Name and First Name Numbers.

The first vowel in your name – A, E, I, O, U or Y – reveals your first emotional reaction. Its sound is believed to echo the soul of a name or word. If your First Vowel is also your First Letter, you may have difficulty making decisions – your emotional and mental reactions may be confused. All the vowels in your name influence your emotions and needs. All the consonants influence your material thinking and hence your chosen outward appearance.

The Last Letter (often called the Capstone) influences how you conclude your affairs; the Middle Letter (sometimes called the Keystone) – this only occurs in names with an odd number of letters – highlights what may at times be a compulsion or obsession or an imbalance of energy. Your Middle and Last Letters are not as important as your First Letter and First Vowel.

THE LETTERS OF CHER

The First Letter is C(3), showing the first mental reaction to be creative, bright and not taking things too seriously. The First Vowel is E(5), showing the first emotional reaction will be to communicate and seek to change things or possibly to seek freedom from restrictions. The Last Letter is R(9); matters would finally be dealt with in a responsive but powerful way. There is no Middle Letter. Notice how these three letters harmonize – they are all odd numbers. The letters need to be considered beside the Vowel, Consonant and Name Numbers – here they are mostly harmonious.

```
          5
    C H E R
    3  8  9
```

THE ALPHABET

A (1) A MENTAL LETTER

It is assertive and aggressive and thrusts its views into the world. This is seen in its shape – pushing upwards. The leader, with original ideas and ambitious plans behind it. It has a quick temper and prefers activity to sitting still.

As First Letter

encourages leadership.

As First Vowel

acts assertively in emotional matters. There is a dislike of interference.

B (2) AN EMOTIONAL LETTER

It is introverted – two parts of the letter are enclosed, indicating shyness at times. It works well in partnership or as a member of a team. It is sensitive and prefers to improve rather than initiate. There is an appreciation of beauty and the arts.

As First Letter
encourages cooperation.

C (3) AN INTUITIVE LETTER

It can express itself well and is outgoing and gregarious – notice how C is open on one side. It gives attention and in turn receives it back. A creative letter with a certain degree of restlessness. Easily thrown off balance. It performs well before the public. Is loving and needs to show it.

As First Letter
encourages creativity.

D (4) A PHYSICAL LETTER

Brings practicality, patience and efficiency to life. It works long and hard for what it wants. Must avoid getting stuck-in-a-rut – see its enclosed shape. It promotes orthodox thinking. Brings a pragmatic view to life.

As First Letter
encourages practicality.

E (5) A PHYSICAL LETTER

Encourages a versatile and adaptable approach. Restless, with a love of travel. It seeks freedom. This is a popular letter. It is open at the side showing ability to communicate but its lines are straight so it is direct in its approach. Sparkling and effervescent.

As First Letter
encourages communication.

As First Vowel
the emotional reaction is quick. If life is boring it changes its interests.

LEFT LETTER D (4) IS A PHYSICAL LETTER, BRINGING PRACTICALITY, PATIENCE AND EFFICIENCY. ALSO A TENDENCY TO STICK TO ORTHODOX IDEAS.

LEFT F (6), AN INTUITIVE LETTER, BRINGS A NEED FOR CREATIVE FULFILMENT AND IS DRAWN TO THE PERFORMING ARTS. AS A FIRST LETTER, IT ENCOURAGES A SENSE OF FUN.

F (6) AN INTUITIVE LETTER

Brings a need to achieve harmony and balance in life. Not as secure as it appears and sometimes ignores practicalities. Is responsible. It needs creative fulfilment in life and is drawn towards the performing arts.

AS FIRST LETTER

encourages fun and friendship.

G (7) A MENTAL LETTER

Has the ability to communicate or withdraw into itself. Often prefers solitude. This is an enigmatic letter with creative potential. It works hard for what it believes in and encourages spirituality. It can be obstinate.

AS FIRST LETTER

encourages self-reliance.

H (8) A MENTAL LETTER

H is materially powerful. It enjoys climbing the ladder of success (look at its shape). It works methodically towards what it wants and has financial acumen. Independent, often desiring social success. Open to new situations and aware of spiritual needs.

AS FIRST LETTER

encourages financial abilities.

I(9) AN EMOTIONAL LETTER

Emotional and independent. It knows what it wants and dislikes interference. Idealistic and impractical with a romantic attitude to life. It can be over-dramatic, impressionable and sensitive. It helps develop humanitarian instincts.

AS FIRST LETTER

encourages idealism.

AS FIRST VOWEL

it reacts in a romantic, idealistic, and impractical way.

J (10/1) A MENTAL LETTER

It has leadership qualities but is not as secure as it first appears. Look at its curved base, it can rock from side to side. It has a strong sense of self and prefers action to inaction. If it proceeds with caution, it achieves its ambitions. It can be inattentive.

AS FIRST LETTER

encourages mental judgement.

K (11/2) AN INTUITIVE LETTER

Inspired thought and the ability to inspire others is given to the name with this letter. It can cooperate but its idealism can sometimes be a problem. It does not like second best. It may create a nervous atmosphere around it.

AS FIRST LETTER

encourages inspiration.

L (12/3) A MENTAL LETTER

Exerts a magnetic attraction. A loving, expressive letter that draws people towards it. L is not serious in its attitude and prefers the lighter side of life. Critical when thwarted. More settled and secure than it appears and has planning ability. It is at ease in social events and gatherings.

AS FIRST LETTER

encourages sociability.

RIGHT L (12/3), A MENTAL LETTER, EXERTS A MAGNETIC ATTRACTION. NOT SERIOUS IN ITS OUTLOOK, IT ENCOURAGES EASE IN SOCIAL SITUATIONS.

M (13/4) A PHYSICAL LETTER

Can be extremely practical but craves love and excitement. It encourages a series of ups and downs in life and can be moody. Strong-willed, but will compromise rather than risk losing all. Conservative and orthodox with good ability to concentrate.

As First Letter

encourages integrity.

N (14/5) A MENTAL LETTER

Enjoys a life of change in which pleasure is not ignored. Sensual, preferring to be around others, occasionally overdosing on the social scene. N helps with public recognition. When self-disciplined, it can attain what it wants. It tends to repeat mistakes.

As First Letter

encourages popularity.

O(15/6) AN EMOTIONAL LETTER

73

Represents the magic circle. 0 is self-contained, studious, and retains what it gains. A good financial letter. Will-power and self-discipline are strong. Like the sun – look at its shape – it attracts attention. It easily adapts to domestic changes.

As First Letter

encourages scholarship.

As First Vowel

aware of the spiritual in daily life. Can become emotionally fatigued.

P (16/7) A MENTAL LETTER

It has intellectual intensity and encourages deep thinking on many aspects of life. Surprising events can occur – conditions overturned or overthrown without warning. Encourages an

RIGHT O (15/6) IS AN EMOTIONAL LETTER. AS A FIRST VOWEL MAY ENCOURAGE EMOTIONAL FATIGUE.

interest in religion, metaphysics or the occult. It dislikes interference intensely.

AS FIRST LETTER

encourages self-knowledge.

Q (17/8) AN INTUITIVE LETTER

Unusual, it adds eccentricity to the name. Financially acute, it has a different and distinctive way of living. It uses its intuition. Q enhances physical prowess. It can make mistakes in judgement but is still a good letter for anyone in business.

AS FIRST LETTER

encourages unorthodoxy.

R (18/9) AN EMOTIONAL LETTER

A letter of power. Humanitarian instincts and a need for action and achievement. In the past, dubbed the 'growling' letter. Self-confident with materialistic and idealistic needs. Creative ventures helped.

AS FIRST LETTER

encourages determination.

S (19/1) AN EMOTIONAL LETTER

Many successes and failures with this letter, many twists and turns – look at its shape. S needs success and social esteem. It encourages ambition in any name. Not always secure and can become too self-absorbed. Powerful and shrewd.

AS FIRST LETTER

encourages ambition.

T (20/2) AN EMOTIONAL LETTER

The letter of the martyr – look at its shape, that of the cross. Loving, tactful and wishing to show friendship. It adds a degree of nervousness to the name. Not always comfortable in competitive situations, preferring to follow rather than lead. It has the ability to teach. It thrives on affection.

AS FIRST LETTER

encourages trust.

U (21/3) AN INTUITIVE LETTER

A joyful and sociable letter. Open to express itself yet easily thrown off-balance. Its shape is open at the top with a base that can rock. It attracts good fortune but can carelessly lose it. A happy letter. Indecisive at times.

AS FIRST LETTER

encourages gregariousness.

AS FIRST VOWEL

the emotional response is loving and passionate, sometimes melodramatic.

V (22/4) AN INTUITIVE LETTER

One of the most powerful letters in the alphabet. It helps manifest far-reaching changes, mapping out its life by constructing dynamic plans that work. Nervous tension overpowers it at times. It can be ruthless.

AS FIRST LETTER

encourages achievement.

W (23/5) A PHYSICAL LETTER

Look at its shape – like the waves of the sea. W has a life of ups and downs. A dizzyingly diverse lifestyle. Communication, adaptability and versatility are all here. It enjoys life to the full. Pleasure and change are needed as much as work. A difficult letter to pin down, but always popular.

AS FIRST LETTER

encourages versatility.

X (24/6) AN EMOTIONAL LETTER

A letter – like most letters at the end of the alphabet – of high voltage. X does not often occur in names. It gives sensuality and helps in public recognition. It can symbolize sacrificing oneself to a cause or belief. Underneath its glamour, it is exacting in its attention to detail.

AS FIRST LETTER

encourages personal magnetism.

Y (25/7) AN INTUITIVE LETTER

This letter faces many choices – look at the way it resembles a fork in a path. Spiritually inspired, it finds it hard to commit itself to a single cause of action. It helps in intellectual work. Works well alone. Psychic and intuitive ability is enhanced with Y.

AS FIRST LETTER

encourages perception.

AS FIRST VOWEL

emotionally indecisive but with strong intuition that can be used successfully.

Z (26/8) AN EMOTIONAL LETTER

Often compared to a flash of forked lightning – look at its design. This letter promotes recognition and fame. There is power and a love of luxury here. An interest in metaphysics or the occult can often be present. A comfortable home-life is important. A good letter financially. Z is usually unconventional.

AS FIRST LETTER

encourages power.

ABOVE Z (26/8) USUALLY ENCOURAGES THE IMPORTANCE OF A COMFORTABLE HOME LIFE. A LOVE OF LUXURY TOO. AS A FIRST LETTER, IT ENCOURAGES POWER.

THE INTENSITY NUMBERS AND NAMECHART

It is with our passions as it is with fire and water, they are good servants but bad masters.

ROGER L'ESTRANGE

Within the name, a number repeated more times than any other is known as the Intensity Number. It shows a hidden desire. It is sometimes called the Ruling or Secret Passion. It can, if dominant, affect the characteristics of the Name, Vowel and Consonant Numbers (see box on p.79). A single Intensity Number can have a strong effect; when there is no Intensity Number, the name is often better balanced.

THE INTENSITY NUMBERS

1 Intensifies the awareness of self. The will is strong and the name encourages assertiveness, originality, and self-confidence. It colours the Name Number with an ability to lead and a degree of initiative.

2 Intensifies a feeling of being in tune with other people. Tact, diplomacy and cooperation with others are encouraged. It colours the Name Number with the characteristic of following rather than leading and adds a sense of rhythm and sensitivity to everything that is attempted.

3 Intensifies a joyful and happy approach to life. It promotes an ability to entertain and share with others the good things in life. Creativity of all kinds is generally enhanced. It colours the Name Number with the art of mixing well, and the ability to socialize. Gregariousness is strengthened.

4 Intensifies a practical and orthodox attitude to living. Enhances the ability to cope with detailed, demanding work and the patience to finish whatever has been started. The Name Number is coloured with a focused and single-minded attitude to work, a degree of workaholism is added.

5 Intensifies the need for freedom and the wish to change constantly. It adds versatility, enhances an awareness of sexual needs and the ability to adapt to quickly changing circumstances. It colours the Name Number with the ability to communicate widely and to motivate other people.

6 Intensifies a feeling of responsibility about life and a need for justice and fairness. Aids creative and vocal work. May encourage a habit of over-eating. The ability to teach and foster the skills of others is enhanced. The Name Number is coloured with an overall sense of harmony and balance.

INTENSITY NUMBERS

Intensity Numbers

1 5	5
M A E	W E S T
4	5 1 2

The 5 is repeated more times than any other number. Mae West would have had an Intensity Number of 5. The Name, Vowel and Consonant Numbers are still the most important – the Intensity adds further information. Mae West was noted for her witty remarks, especially relating to sex, and 5 is the number of sexual magnetism. Her Name Number was also 5 – further strengthened by this Intensity.

7 Intensifies a need for solitude. Use of analysis and intuition is encouraged. Being taught by others is often disliked. Personal experience is important – necessary to make one's own mistakes. Metaphysical interests are likely and it colours the Name Number with mystery.

8 Intensifies the development of a businesslike and efficient attitude. Dependability and organizing ability are enhanced. Financial acumen is strong. Physical interests, sport and so on, can be encouraged. It colours the Name Number with power and the need for success.

9 Intensifies the development of a compassionate and tolerant attitude. There is a dramatic intensity and emotional magnetism attached to this number. A love of travel, romance and the holding of humanitarian and idealistic views are all strengthened. A broad-minded outlook colours the Name Number.

THE MISSING NUMBERS

Any number from 1 to 9 that does not appear in your name
represents a missing quality; if this number does not appear
elsewhere, you will have to consciously develop it.

Numerologists who believe the name on the birth certificate is
all-important regard a missing number as having karmic
implications. The number represents a lesson to be learnt in this
life. If the number is not elsewhere (the Birth Numbers, Vowel,
Consonant, Name or First Name) you will have to develop it.

```
    6           9
  J O H N
  S M I T H
  1  8 5      1 4  2
  8
```

The following name, a fairly
common one, has the numbers
3 and 7 missing. If found
nowhere else, the person using
this name would need to work
harder than most to develop
these qualities.

MEANING OF MISSING NUMBERS

1 Originality is missing. The person needs to develop initiative, the
ability to lead, self-confidence, self-assurance, ambition, a strong
will-power and determination.

2 Sensitivity is missing. The person needs to develop the ability to
cooperate with others, to follow directions, show friendliness,
kindness and awareness of the feelings of others.

3 Creativity is missing. The person needs to develop a less serious
outlook, a joy for living, behave gregariously, have a sense of
humour, be optimistic, and use the imagination.

4 Patience is missing. The person needs to develop practicality, stability, tenacity, attention to detail, the ability to work long and hard, a constructive outlook, a degree of self-discipline.

5 Versatility is missing. The person needs to develop adaptability, a willingness to try anything new, not be afraid of progress, learn how to communicate, to show enthusiasm, to motivate others, to be adventurous.

6 Responsibility is missing. The person needs to be creative and develop a well-balanced outlook, an appreciation of beauty and the arts, a sense of honour, to be able to harmonize divergent aspects of life, to learn how to teach.

7 Self-examination is missing. The person needs to develop spiritual awareness, to gain self-reliance, to be unafraid of solitude, to use intuition and analysis, to learn by experience, to develop inner strength.

8 Financial acumen is missing. The person needs to develop efficiency, dependability, the ability to organize, to help others in need, to develop physical stamina, to be independent, and to be able to use power wisely.

9 Generosity is missing. The person needs to develop humanitarian instincts, compassion, to be broad-minded and tolerant, use creativity, be unafraid of the romantic and the dramatic, to learn how to love without seeking reward.

THE NAMECHART

The numbers of your name can be placed in the same positions as on the Birthchart (*see* chapter 3). You will find it interesting to compare both of these charts. If your Birthchart is weak, with many missing numbers (this will be especially so after 2000 AD, showing the need for those born at the start of the new millennium to consciously develop and grow), a good Namechart will provide you with additional strength. Any imbalance caused by missing numbers on the Birthchart is somewhat eliminated when the numbers appear on the Namechart.

Your Namechart may provide too much strength if it duplicates the Birthchart numbers. It will not then be considered 'balanced', but it can create a charismatic or strong type of person. It is better if any missing Birthchart numbers are present on the Namechart. It makes life more balanced and easier.

82

2	5 5 5 5 5 5	
1 1		

LEFT CHART FOR TENNESSEE WILLIAMS.

Place the numbers contained within your first name on the Namechart first. This is your most important individual name, so its effect is the most striking. In the charts for Tennessee Williams and Zsa Zsa Gabor (p.83) their first names dramatically intensify the Namechart. These names would encourage their possessors to display distinctive attributes. They would not guarantee fame to anyone else, but the effect felt from the name would be similar.

The vibrations from all those 5s in Tennessee (six in a nine-letter name) would assist communication, sexuality – all five senses enhanced; the name Zsa Zsa has strong concentration on the number 1 (four in a six letter name), encouraging leadership and originality, backed by the material power of the number 8. Obviously, the person's other numerological combinations have to be considered.

LEFT CHART FOR ZSA ZSA GABOR.

		8 8
1 1		
1 1		

Now place your last or other names on the chart and compare your Namechart with your Birthchart. Does it over-strengthen certain numbers? The Birthchart and Namechart of the American playwright, Eugene O'Neill on p.84 show how his Namechart and Birthchart compliment each other; combined, he had only the 2 and 4 as missing numbers. This is a powerful name that balances well the numbers of birth.

Always remember, the name is an outside influence and will never create the strength represented by your birth date and Life Path.

THE SUBMERGED CHARACTERISTIC

The Submerged Characteristic is a less important number. It is hidden most of the time and you will use it only occasionally when problems cannot easily be solved. It is found by adding together the number of letters you have in your complete name. Not the value of the letters but how many you have.

George Bush has ten letters in his name – 10, 1 + 0 = 1 – his Submerged Characteristic is 1; Golda Meir had nine letters, her Submerged Characteristic was 9.

MEANING OF THE SUBMERGED CHARACTERISTIC

1 An original approach will be found. This will take others by surprise. A determination to take the initiative brings speedy results.

2 The ability to let others lead. Collaboration can be successful. Diplomatic skills are in evidence.

3 Imagination and creativity are used when problems seem insoluble. There will be an artistic approach. Difficulties are not always taken very seriously.

4 Realistic objectives will be approached logically. Detailed analysis will be employed. A practical and orthodox solution will be preferred. Uninvolved emotionally.

5 The ability to accept change. A new, untried solution can succeed. Risks will be taken. Quickness and versatility surfaces.

6 Responsible decisions taking account of all involved will be employed. The effect on family life will be considered.

	6	
		8 8 8
1 1 1		

ABOVE EUGENE O'NEILL'S BIRTHCHART (10. 16. 1888).

7 Solutions are found within oneself. There is a disinclination to take advice. The person will not want to act until conditions are perfect. Meditative.

8 Efficiency can be used in a ruthless manner. Definite results and goals will be the aim of any problem solving.

9 A broad-minded view will be taken. Generous towards others. Idealistic in approach. If opposed, reactions can be unexpected and dramatic.

3 3 3	6	9
	5 5 5 5 5 5	
		7

ABOVE EUGENE O'NEILL'S NAMECHART.

THE TEMPERAMENT CHART

CHAPTER TEN

No, Groucho is not my real name. I'm breaking it in for a friend.

GROUCHO MARX

The letters in your name affect the way you carry out your plans. Two people may have the same Name Number but the letters behind it show how they prefer to express themselves – either mentally, physically, emotionally or intuitively. To find this we use the Temperament Chart.

	Mental	Physical	Emotional	Intuitive
Starters	A	E	I O R Z	K
Improvers	H J N P	W	B S T X	F Q U Y
Finishers	G L	D M		C V

ABOVE THE TEMPERAMENT CHART.

The Mental Letters indicate a thinking approach. Decisions are made coolly and calmly. A majority of letters here does not, unfortunately, make you a genius – but you will always think things out before acting.

The Physical Letters show a need for taking action rather than sitting around thinking. A majority of letters here indicates promotion of energy, keeping busy. The person needs to act rather than consider.

The Emotional Letters show the heart and dreams are always considered. A majority of letters here indicates decisions based on desire. Artistic awareness is present.

The Intuitive Letters show instinct is always relied on. There is a degree of psychic awareness. Names containing a majority of intuitive letters help develop a knowledge of the spirit. There is often a dreamlike quality about this person.

If a section has considerably more letters than any other, this part of your temperament will be stronger. If there is an even spread in all four sections, then your name and temperament are well-balanced.

From the Temperament, you can see which type of career your name ideally helps. Most letters in the Mental section assist cerebral or sedentary work. The Physical section promotes physical or practical work. The Emotional helps artistic or creative careers: the theatre, fashion or creative hobbies. The Intuitive Letters assist unorthodox types of employment or spiritual or religious careers.

The letters are also divided into three sections: Starters, Improvers and Finishers. Where you have the most letters shows how your name helps you begin, continue or finish projects.

Place all your letters in their respective positions on the chart. Add together the amount of letters (fadically) contained separately in each section. As an example, look at the chart for the name of the French writer, Jean-Paul Sartre (p.87). Notice the dominance of the number 7 (the deep thinker) in both the Mental and Starter sections. Here is someone who will have a clear intellectual view about what he is doing in life. He will follow his mind rather than his heart. The 7 shows a concern with the inner meaning of life. His emotional

	Mental	Physical	Emotional	Intuitive	
Starters	A A A	E E	R R		7
Improvers	J N P		S T	U	6
Finishers	L				1
	7	2	4	1	

ABOVE JEAN-PAUL SARTRE'S TEMPERAMENT CHART.

feelings will be dealt with in a practical way – here he has a 4. Physically he has a 2 and should be able to cooperate in everyday affairs; intuition comes in an inspired way – the number 1.

He is able to initiate projects and continue with them once started. Although he can finish what he begins, the single 1 in the Finisher section indicates difficulties at times.

THE TEMPERAMENT NUMBERS

NUMBER 1

MENTAL An original thinker with the ability to conceive new and exciting ways of doing things but can dominate discussions sometimes. May show impatience.

PHYSICAL Can show leadership qualities. There is a need to keep busy. Active, with a sense of humour. Can be brusque.

EMOTIONAL Prefers to be the dominant partner in a relationship. Has an optimistic and original outlook. There may be a dislike of psychoanalysis.

INTUITIVE New and original ideas may appear as if from nowhere. May have good creative instincts which can be used with enthusiasm.

NUMBER 2

MENTAL Enjoys collecting knowledge and is good at detailed work. Finds it easy to collaborate or work with others and can see both sides of the question.

PHYSICAL Can work easily as part of a team. Is able to improve things that others have started. May have artistic hobbies or interests.

EMOTIONAL Has a need for companionship. Feels lost without somebody to share with. Extremely sensitive to the needs of others and is over-sensitive at times.

INTUITIVE Uses intuition easily and is sensitive to atmosphere. This number helps psychic qualities unfold. Spiritually aware. Hesitant.

NUMBER 3

MENTAL Brings creativity to any mental problem and life is not always taken seriously. A sense of the absurd. Needs constant stimulation.

PHYSICAL Self-expressive and artistic. Often a popular person with joie de vivre. Easily bored. Restlessness and carelessness can be shown.

EMOTIONAL Can easily express desires, dreams and love. Likes receiving affection and wants it to be shown. Witty, with creative talents. Moves on when bored.

INTUITIVE Instinct and intuition are used creatively. Imaginative and artistic in feelings. There can be an attraction towards ritual.

NUMBER 4

MENTAL Uses logic to approach any mental problem. Is practical and orthodox. Distrusts anything too original.

PHYSICAL Can work hard and feels uneasy with nothing to do. May have a talent for using the hands in some way.

EMOTIONAL Practical matters are always considered. Is serious in emotions. Can be loyal. There may be a feeling of restriction.

INTUITIVE Either distrusts the inner voice, or feels more comfortable following a logical, practical path. Orthodox in religion or agnostic.

NUMBER 5

MENTAL A quick and versatile mind. No restrictions on interests. Bright conversationalist. May change interests suddenly. Attracted to things that are new.

PHYSICAL Works well with others. Active and athletic with a competitive instinct. Adapts well to change and copes extremely well in a crisis.

EMOTIONAL Seeks freedom and dislikes being tied down. Changes interests and affections easier than most. Popular, adventurous and exciting.

INTUITIVE Attuned to the reactions of others. Good instincts but often distrusts them and may need proof before acting.

NUMBER 6

MENTAL Brings responsibility to the thinking process. Can be a creative problem-solver. Understands the difficulties of others.

PHYSICAL Balances work and home life equally and needs both. Works well with or for others. Needs to have beauty around. Can show creativity.

EMOTIONAL Artistic interests are important but will sacrifice much for a stable domestic background. Can accept responsibility easily.

INTUITIVE

Must trust instinct more than trusting other people. Keeps a good balance between intuition and fact. Inclined to meddle.

NUMBER 7

MENTAL Needs solitude to make decisions. Good analytical ability. Sees a lot but keeps silent. Dislikes interference in decision making.

PHYSICAL Active, but prefers working alone to being part of a team. Dislikes a noisy or crowded environment. Puzzling to others.

RIGHT THE PHYSICAL ASPECT OF TEMPERAMENT NUMBER 5 IS ACTIVE AND ATHLETIC WITH A COMPETITIVE INSTINCT. EMOTIONALLY, SEEKS ADVENTURE AND DISLIKES RESTRICTION.

EMOTIONAL Capable of deep emotional commitment but dislikes others knowing this. A need to achieve perfection in everything.

INTUITIVE A strong inner voice that needs to be acted on; sometimes it is ignored. Good evaluation of others' needs. Spiritually strong.

NUMBER 8

MENTAL Powerful and efficient business sense. A need to succeed. Strong and tough debater. Has to beware of materialistic greed.

PHYSICAL Athletic ability enhanced. Becomes a prominent figure in any team-work. Realistic and dependable.

EMOTIONAL Career interests usually put first. Will try to dominate in relationships. Staunch ally in a crisis or in a time of need.

INTUITIVE Can use intuition to help others less fortunate. Is able to mix spirituality with materialism to good effect.

NUMBER 9

MENTAL Has a wide vision of what needs to be done. Dislikes dealing with details. Idealistic. Humanitarian values kept in mind.

PHYSICAL Dramatic and artistic expression usually preferred. Brings an inspired approach to mundane and routine matters. Shows compassion to others.

EMOTIONAL Romantic and deep feelings are affected by this number. Melodramatic at times – up one minute, down the next. Can be too trusting.

INTUITIVE Attuned to a higher consciousness. Inspired dreams may sometimes create impracticality. Strong spiritual beliefs.

ZERO ON THE TEMPERAMENT CHART

MENTAL A dislike of taking decisions (or making them) based on fact. Lack of confidence in using logical thought. Difficulty studying.

PHYSICAL Physical stamina and endurance is not marked. There can be difficulty in dealing with life in a practical manner. May need motivating.

EMOTIONAL Emotional feeling is repressed or there is a difficulty in expressing it. Life seems dull at times. Understands others with difficulty.

INTUITIVE A disinclination to follow hunches or instincts. Lack of interest in the spiritual world or metaphysical topics. Has difficulty coping with the abstract.

LOOKING FOR HARMONY IN YOUR NUMBERS

Your two most important numbers are your Life Path and Name Number. As stated earlier, if they are the same, you have the perfect combination. The next best combination is if they are both odd or both even – with this there is still harmony. If one is odd and the other even there is conflict; although life is not so smooth it provides opportunities to grow stronger as you surmount any problems.

COMBINATIONS AND HARMONY

A quick and easy way to see the general harmony of your life is to compare your Life Path, Name and Power (remembering the Power Number is found by adding the Life Path and Name Numbers together). For example:

Life Path 4 Name 4 Power 8 = a perfect combination

Life Path 2 Name 6 Power 8 = a harmonious combination

Life Path 3 Name 4 Power 7 = a conflicting combination

More detail is acquired by comparing all your main numbers. Your Life Path is the key. If other numbers do not conflict with your Life Path success comes easier; future difficulties are easier to cope with.

If the Name Number conflicts, but the other numbers are harmonious, there may still be dissatisfaction felt in what is being achieved. Achievement refers to not only material success but spiritual and emotional as well.

To assess your main characteristics, use only the following numbers: Life Path (LP); Birthday (B); Goal (G); Name Number (N); Vowel Number (V); Consonant Number (C); First Name (FN); First Letter (FL); First Vowel (FV); Power (P); and your Intensity Number (I) – but only if your Intensity is represented by a single number, not two or three.

Write down your numbers on a piece of paper from 1 to 9 in a line placing your main numbers underneath. Use initial letters to indicate the names of the numbers. Shown below are the numbers of the former British Prime Minister, Margaret Thatcher. She was born on 13 October 1925.

MARGARET THATCHER

1	2	3	4	5	6	7	8	9
FV1	FN2		LP4	G5			P8	C9
			B4					
			N4					
			V4					
			FL4					

There is no single Intensity Number. This is an excellent chart. Observe the strong support for her 4 Life Path. Accepting the opportunities for hard work and self-discipline that the 4 Life Path brings would be not be difficult for a person with these numbers supporting the chart.

THE CYCLE AND YEAR NUMBERS

CHAPTER ELEVEN

When one has much to put into them,
a day has a hundred pockets.
FRIEDRICH NIETZSCHE

The opportunities that occur in your life appear in cycles. Numerology can show this but it does not make predictions; it does not tell your fortune. But it can show the probable events and opportunities you will encounter.

Your full birth date is the foundation the cycles in your life have developed from. You have many different cycles all occurring at the same time. This chapter and the following one will show how to find the most important.

THE THREE CYCLES OF LIFE

Your life is divided into three stages or cycles. The first is represented by the fadic number of your month of birth; the second, by the fadic number of your day of birth; the third by the number of your birth year after using fadic addition.

Dates in America are written with the month first; in Britain, with the birth day first. In this chapter, the American system will be used; this is the conventional way to calculate cycles in numerology. Wherever you were born, for the following calculations always use this order: Birth Month, Birth Day, Birth Year.

Your First Cycle begins when you are born. To find when your Second Cycle starts, you deduct your Life Path Number from the number 36 (this number, 36, which is 9 multiplied by 4, has a powerful occult symbolism attached to it). Your Second Cycle lasts 27 years (9 multiplied by 3) and is followed by your Third Cycle, which lasts until death or until Samuel Butler's description of this transition happens: '. . . a larger kind of going abroad'.

Each cycle shows the general trend behind a part of your life.

THE CYCLES OF LIFE

Life Path 1: Second Cycle begins at 35, Third Cycle at 62

Life Path 2: Second Cycle begins at 34, Third Cycle at 61

Life Path 3: Second Cycle begins at 33, Third Cycle at 60

Life Path 4: Second Cycle begins at 32, Third Cycle at 59

Life Path 5: Second Cycle begins at 31, Third Cycle at 58

Life Path 6: Second Cycle begins at 30, Third Cycle at 57

Life Path 7: Second Cycle begins at 29, Third Cycle at 56

Life Path 8: Second Cycle begins at 28, Third Cycle at 55

Life Path 9: Second Cycle begins at 27, Third Cycle at 54

CYCLE NUMBERS

CYCLE 1 A need to stand on one's own feet. Events instil a degree of independence. The person considers his or her own needs. Impatience is felt at times. New opportunities often occur. Leadership will be conferred at some time – even if unwanted.

CYCLE 2 Opportunities to mix with groups, to work in large organizations or become attached to teams. The person is sensitive to the opinions of others. There are many friends and public recognition can occur, although often unsought. There is a need for companion-ship. Events develop slowly. The person may have to follow the path of others.

CYCLE 3 A pleasant cycle in which creative work can prosper, although there is a likelihood opportunities may be squandered in order to have a good time. The social scene dominates the life. An enjoyment of entertaining or mixing with others is present. The person appears 'lucky'. Restlessness and boredom often occur.

CYCLE 4 Practical matters need to be tackled. There is a good deal of hard work. The person feels restricted at times. The opportunity occurs to lay steady foundations for progress at work or at home. The person needs to relax or play more. Life is taken seriously. Life is busy. A need to guard against getting into a rut.

CYCLE 5 Circumstances change frequently. Surprising adventures occur – often unlooked for. There is difficulty staying in one career. Interests can change. The person will display adaptability. Communicating with others is important. Travel and opportunities to try 'anything new' are available. Competitive situations dominate.

CYCLE 6 There are many creative opportunities during this cycle but the attention may be focused on the domestic environment, which is either harmonious or disruptive. Responsibility is taken on. The person is often asked for advice. A need for love in the life. Searching for 'balance' at all times.

CYCLE 7 There is a lot of inner searching or psychoanalysing of oneself in this cycle. The person feels confused in noisy or bustling environments and there is a need for solitude. Much personal growth can take place. Opportunities occur suddenly. Action is quickly taken after much thought. The person can reject advice and create difficulties.

CYCLE 8 Slow and steady progress is made towards personal goals but the work needs to be done. This is a good financial cycle, but only if it is earned. A tendency to be to demanding and over-ambitious at times. Independence is important. There is a karmic feel to this cycle – good or bad – the person gets what is deserved. Effort is usually needed from the individual.

CYCLE 9 Anything is possible under this number. It is good for creative matters, especially the serious arts. Often there is difficulty in starting new projects; sometimes unaccountable endings. This is an emotional cycle and restraint is needed sometimes. Practical matters need more attention. Travel and a wide circle of friends or contacts are indicated.

THE CHALLENGE NUMBERS

0 CHALLENGE There is no individual Challenge present. This does not mean that there is no individual negative quality to overcome – only that it will constantly change.

1 CHALLENGE There is reluctance to take a leadership role, to take the initiative. There is a fear of independence.

2 CHALLENGE There is a lack of awareness of the needs of others. A disinclination to cooperate. A lack of sensitivity.

3 CHALLENGE There is a reluctance to enjoy life or be frivolous. Creativity may be squandered. A difficulty in self-expression.

4 CHALLENGE There is a dislike of looking at life realistically or in a practical way. There is difficulty in getting out of a rut.

RIGHT WITH THE 4 CHALLENGE THERE MAY BE DIFFICULTY IN BEING REALISTIC AND MOVING ON FROM OLD THINGS.

THE CHALLENGE

Behind each individual cycle is a Challenge: this shows self-imposed restrictions that must be conquered to attain fulfilment.

The First Challenge operates during the First Cycle; the Second Challenge is in force during the Second Cycle; the Third Challenge is the most important – it operates during the Third Cycle but its restrictions are felt throughout the life. As we age, the challenges have less power. They have usually already been acknowledged and conquered.

The First Challenge is found by subtracting your fadic Month Number from your Birthday Number (or the smaller from the larger); the Second Challenge by subtracting your Birthday from your fadic Year of Birth Number; the Third Challenge by subtracting your First Challenge Number from your Second Challenge Number.

This birth date, 11. 22. 1943, belongs to the tennis player, Billie Jean King. After fadic addition her birth date looks like this: 2. 4. 8. Her First Challenge is 2 (4 – 2 = 2); her Second Challenge is 4 (8 – 4 = 4); her Third Challenge is 2 (4 – 2 = 2).

5 CHALLENGE There is a fear of the new, of taking a risk. There will be a lack of interest in communicating with others.

6 CHALLENGE There is the possibility of disruption in domestic concerns unless a balance is attained. A dislike of responsibility.

7 CHALLENGE There is a dislike of solitude. A fear of examining one's own motives. A lack of faith.

8 CHALLENGE There is a reluctance to accept personal power. The life feels disjointed. There is greed.

THE TURNING POINTS

There are four Turning Points in your life. Significant events occur at these times. Sometimes they will not be recognized as such until later. During these Turning Points you have a heightened inner energy. This helps you to meet your opportunities in a positive manner. The First Point is found by deducting your Life Path Number from the number 36 (it is the same age as the beginning of your Second Cycle). Your next three Turning Points occur every nine years after that.

The Turning Point lasts for one year but its effects can be experienced over a longer period of time. It can be felt up to one year before it begins and the effects can last for three to four years after, although the full potent effect will be felt during its first year of transit.

NUMBER VIBRATIONS
FOR TURNING POINTS

First Turning Point: add the numbers of your Birth Month and Birthday together fadically.

Second Turning Point: add the numbers of your Birthday and Birth Year together fadically.

Third Turning Point: add the numbers of your First and Second Points together fadically.

Fourth Turning Point: add your Birth Month and Birth Year together fadically.

For example: the numbers of the Turning Points in the life of the actor Marlon Brando, who was born 4. 3. 1924 (4. 3. 7), are:

his First was 7 (4 + 3 = 7)

his Second was 1 (3 + 7 = 10, 1 + 0 = 1)

his Third was 8 (7 + 1 = 8)

his Fourth was 2 (4 + 7 = 11, 1 + 1 = 2)

THE TURNING POINTS OCCUR AT THE FOLLOWING AGES:

Life Path 1: at ages 35, 44, 53 and 62

Life Path 2: at ages 34, 43, 52 and 61

Life Path 3: at ages 33, 42, 51 and 60

Life Path 4: at ages 32, 41, 50 and 59

Life Path 5: at ages 31, 40, 49 and 58

Life Path 6: at ages 30, 39, 48 and 57

Life Path 7: at ages 29, 38, 47 and 56

Life Path 8: at ages 28, 37, 46 and 55

Life Path 9: at ages 27, 36, 45 and 54

TURNING POINT NUMBERS

TURNING POINT 1 A new direction in life appears. There is the opportunity to gain independence. The person is concerned with personal needs.

TURNING POINT 2 A partnership can begin. There is a need to mix with people. Psychic ability is enhanced and the person is aware of the needs of others.

TURNING POINT 3 Pleasure and social events dominate. Travel is likely. The mental and creative powers are used fully.

TURNING POINT 4 There is much work but it is coped with easily. An opportunity to lay strong foundations for the rest of the life occurs.

TURNING POINT 5 Something new and completely unexpected appears in the life. A need for freedom is felt. A progressive opportunity should be grasped.

TURNING POINT 6 Creative matters come to the fore. A lot of interest is centred on the home. Responsibilities are easily handled. Love, marriage or divorce is possible.

TURNING POINT 7 Individuality is strengthened and personal motivation is better understood. Opportunities occur out of the blue. A mysterious time that is understood better afterwards.

TURNING POINT 8 Material success can be attained. Opportunities to gain independence can be earned. A good time financially.

TURNING POINT 9 An established part of the life can end. There is a great change, often confusion, often travel. The person is highly emotional but emerges stronger and more compassionate after it is over.

UNIVERSAL YEAR, MONTH AND DAY

The Universal Year Number is the number of each year after using fadic addition. The Universal Year Number for 1999 is 1 (1 + 9 + 9 + 9 = 28, 2 + 8 = 10, 1 + 0 = 1); the Universal Year Number for 2000 is 2 (2 + 0 + 0 + 0 = 2).

To find the Universal Month you add the calendar number of the month in question to the Universal Year Number: December 1999 is 4 (1 + 2 + 1 = 4).

The Universal Day is (either the calendar day added to the Universal Month or) the fadic total of the full date: 31 December 1999 is 8 (3 + 1 + 1 + 2 + 1 + 9 + 9 + 9 = 35, 3 + 5 = 8).

The last day of the millennium is 8, once known as the 'number of karma' (we receive what we deserve), and the first Universal Day of the year 2000 is a 4 (a chance to lay firm foundations for the future).

For matters, projects and interests for which you need the cooperation of others – anything that you cannot put into operation without using the help of others – you will need to consider the Universal Day.

Using the day when the universal vibrations will help you is wise. The Universal Day that matches your Life Path Number is considered 'lucky' for you.

THE EFFECTS OF THE UNIVERSAL VIBRATIONS

1 Vibration: New starts, opportunities, independence, starting anew.

2 Vibration: A quiet time, consolidating, cooperating, teamwork.

3 Vibration: Entertainment, self-expression, sociability, travel.

4 Vibration: Laying plans, practicality, organization, working hard.

5 Vibration: Exciting changes, freedom, communication, travel, sexual attraction.

6 Vibration: Home activities, creativity, responsibilities, marriage.

7 Vibration: Inner searching, study, rest, unexpected surprises.

8 Vibration: Material success or failure, independence, goals set can be achieved.

9 Vibration: Humanitarian matters, idealism, endings, high drama.

PERSONAL YEAR, MONTH AND DAY

Your Personal Year starts on the 1st January each year (although you will feel its vibrations from October onward of the preceding year; it will continue to operate, weakening, into the following year until the start of a 1 Personal Month). To find its number, add your Birthday and Month Numbers together (this is, as you will have realized, your Goal Number) to the year in question. For example: if your Birthday and Month are 5 and 5, and you wanted to find out what opportunities 1999 would bring – you would add 5 + 5 + 1 + 9 + 9 + 9 = 38, 3 + 8 = 11, 1 + 1 = 2. 1999 would be a 2 Personal Year for you.

To find your Personal Month Number, add the calendar number of the month to your Personal Year Number. To find December for the above 2 Personal Year, you would add 12 and 2, 1 + 2 + 2 = 5. December in 1999 would be a 5 Personal Month.

To find your Personal Day Number, add the number of the day to your Personal Month. In the above example, 31st December would be 3 + 1 + 5 = 9. A 9 Personal Day.

For someone with a 5 Birthday and 5 Birth Month Number, the date 12. 31. 1999 would work out as a 2 Personal Year, 5 Personal Month and a 9 Personal Day. All three numbers would be operating on a personal level for that person on that day. The Universal vibrations should not, of course, be forgotten.

PERSONAL VIBRATIONS

PERSONAL 1 VIBRATION A time to begin life anew. The ability to start afresh. New directions and opportunities are offered and should be accepted. A self-confident phase. An energizing time.

PERSONAL 2 VIBRATION A peaceful and calm period after the 1. There is time to think and consolidate plans. It is easier than usual to cooperate with others. Sensitivity is enhanced. Affection and love are felt.

PERSONAL 3 VIBRATION A happy, joyous period. Imaginative affairs and creative use of the mind prosper. Travel is likely. There are many opportunities to mingle and socialize. There is an element of good luck.

RIGHT THE CHINESE CHARACTER FOR PEACE IS IN FULL ACCORD WITH THE PERSONAL 2 VIBRATION. A TIME TO THINK AND CONSOLIDATE PLANS.

PERSONAL 4 VIBRATION Patience and organization pay off. A practical, stable period when the opportunity to build stronger foundations for what has already been established prevails.

PERSONAL 5 VIBRATION Change is in the air. Freedom is sought. New people or interests come into the life. Under this number adaptability is stronger than usual. There are many sensual attractions. A second chance (after 1) to start afresh.

PERSONAL 6 VIBRATION Domestic matters occupy a lot of time. The best number for love or marriage. Responsibilities are taken on more willingly than usual. Creative endeavours are favoured.

PERSONAL 7 VIBRATION Important insight into one's own motives occurs. There is a stronger need than usual to spend time alone. Frustration can be experienced materially and then, when least expected, surprising victories occur.

PERSONAL 8 VIBRATION Success and material achievement can be gained if they have been worked for. A good business vibration. Independence is won. A balance between the material and spiritual brings success.

PERSONAL 9 VIBRATION Unlooked for endings occur – but only of what is no longer needed. The dross is shifted from the life. Opportunities to show compassion and understanding appear. An emotional and dramatic time. Idealistic and romantic. Travel can feature. A number of fulfilment but not especially good for new starts – make plans to begin again in 1.

In practice you may find the Personal Year and Personal Month an accurate guide to your opportunities for the month and year; the Universal Day reliable for instigating action on a daily basis; the Personal Day instructive for inner needs.

THE TRANSIT AND EVENT NUMBERS

CHAPTER TWELVE

There's a divinity that shapes our ends,
rough-hew them how we will.
WILLIAM SHAKESPEARE

Forecasts can be made relating to events in your life by using your full birth name – this is the name as written on your birth certificate. There are many things in life we cannot explain or scientifically prove – from intuition to religious belief – and it is necessary sometimes to keep an open mind. You will be able to examine your past life with this technique and prove to yourself if it works or not.

The full name on your birth certificate is needed even if it is a name you no longer use. Each letter in your name affects your life for a particular year or years. The letters (as used in this way) are called the Letters of Transit.

Write down your full name (exactly as written on the birth certificate even if there are misspellings or extraneous words) with the number values of the letters on top. As an example, see the box for Ann Rose Smith on p.107. It is possible to set up a chart for a new name if you know the exact year the name was taken. But the complete birth name will always still apply. The name you are known by, if it is harmonious with your Life Path, will ease difficult transits; a conflicting name does not help. The Letters of Transit operate from birthday to birthday, not from the 1st of January as the Personal Year does.

Two or more of the same letters (for instance: two As) transiting at the same time may create a strong but difficult period. Care should be taken over calculating the transits. It is simple to do but mistakes are common. A single error will disrupt your forecasting.

THE LETTERS OF TRANSIT

A (1 YEAR) Change, new starts, beginnings. A change of direction in the career, or a change of home. Creative projects begun.
AA Over-active. May miss opportunities.

B (2 YEARS) A slower pace is indicated. Partnerships or love affairs favoured. Excessive nervousness possible and health needs watching.
BB An over-emotional period.

C (3 YEARS) Creativity enhanced. Social events are highlighted. Domestic disharmony is possible. An enjoyable time but restless.
CC Play too hard. Extremely restless.

D (4 YEARS) Opportunities to organize and take responsibility for one's own life. Practical, hard-working period. Rest is needed.
DD Workaholism. Life seems limited.

E (5 YEARS) Freedom is sought. Exciting changes and meeting of new people. A possible opportunity for travel and new love affairs. Period of eccentricity.
EE Changing of ideas and interests too often.

F (6 YEARS) Responsibilities taken on. A good financial period. Domestic matters become important. Romantic interests possible.
FF Overburdened with responsibilities.

G (7 YEARS) Solitude needed at times. Tendency to secrecy. Finances good. Excellent period for study or research.
GG Spending too much time alone.

H (8 YEARS) Good period for business expansion. Financial trend is upwards. Can try too hard. Can establish independence.
HH Over-ambitious at work.

I (9 YEARS) An emotional period. Nervousness and delays are possible. Many dramatic ups and downs may occur. Opportunities for creativity always present.
II Difficulty in getting things started.

J(1 YEAR) A change of some sort. Financial prospects good. Indecision at times.
JJ Over-activity leads to confusion.

K (2 YEARS) Spiritually inspiring period. Partnerships are enhanced. Health may need attention. Unusual events.
KK Emotionally sensitive.

L (3 YEARS) Many new friends and social events. Good for creative purposes but may waste opportunities having fun.
LL Over-indulging in pleasure.

M (4 YEARS) Practical and realistic time. Needing to work hard. Finances improve slowly. Energy levels not high.
MM Over-work. Rest needed.

LETTERS OF TRANSIT

1 5 5	9 6 1 5	1 4 9 2 8
A N N	R O S E	S M I T H

Each letter transits your life for the same number of years as its value (A being 1 would be activated for one year; N being 5 would be activated for 5 years). After the transits of all the letters in a name you return to the first letter to repeat the process. Each individual name is analysed separately: Ann, Rose and Smith are treated individually and not together as Ann Rose Smith.

The transits begin on the day you are born. Place O under each first letter. Your second letter starts after the required number of years of your first letter has ended. In our example, A being 1 transits for the first twelve months of life (1 year) and N starts at the first birthday.

1	5	5		9	6	1	5		1	4	9	2	8
A	N	N		R	O	S	E		S	M	I	T	H
0	1	6		0	9	15	16		0	1	5	14	16
11	12	17		21	30	36	37		24	25	29	38	40
22	23	28		42	51	57	58		48	49	53	62	64
33	34	39		63	72	78	79		72	73	77	86	88

Looking at Ann Rose Smith (with three names she will always have three letters in transit at any one time), we see the A of Ann affected her first year; the R of Rose influenced her first nine years; and the S of Smith was in operation for her first year of life (or until she had the S again at twenty-four years of age).

If we wanted to find the likely events she would encounter aged eighteen, we would refer to her name and see that N, E and H were then in transit.

N (5 YEARS) Pleasurable period with exciting events. Travel indicated. Many changes possible. Adaptability enhanced. Finances fluctuate.
NN Extreme restlessness.

O (6 YEARS) Good period to study in. Domestic responsibilities accepted. Finances improve. A calm, sure, period.
OO Emotionally drained by the problems of others.

P (7 YEARS) Intellectual activities enhanced. Time spent alone is needed. Good business vibration if precautions taken.
PP Behave at times too much like a hermit.

Q (8 YEARS) Unusual business ventures favoured. Misunderstood by others.
QQ Judged as over-eccentric.

R (9 YEARS) Creative and compassionate period. Ambitions highlighted. Much confusion and emotion present. Delays at times.
RR Endings and delays. A difficult time.

S (1 YEAR) Circumstances change. Surprises. Often emotions are high. An active and ambitious period.
SS Reversals likely.

T (2 YEARS) Possible change of home. Partnerships prosper. Health needs watching. More sensitive and aware than usual.
TT Over-tense.

U (3 YEARS) Creative time. Enjoyable experiences associated with groups. Financial acumen is low. Confidence needs boosting.

LEFT TWO LETTERS TRANSITING AT THE SAME TIME MAY CREATE A DIFFICULT PERIOD. TWO Ts ARE LIKELY TO INCREASE TENSION

UU Confusion.

V (4 YEARS) Important practical venture started. Personal power is marked during this period. Hard working is probable. Possibility of outstanding achievement.
VV Plans too ambitious. Overworked.

W (5 YEARS) Many changes happen. An adventurous period. Emotions need restraining. Travel likely. Interests change quickly.
WW Scatters energy over many interests.

X (6 YEARS) Home life enhanced. An unusual period. Public recognition possible. Romantic and love interests high.
XX Accept sacrifices in some way.

Y (7 YEARS) A need to choose a direction. Solitude needed to make life decisions. Spiritual awareness gained after confusion.
YY Inability to take positive action.

Z (8 YEARS) Fine financial prospects. Business ability enhanced. Unusual or psychic affairs attract. Unusual domestic conditions.
ZZ Difficult domestic situations.

Note: Two or more Rs in transit during the same year can cause considerable delays; two or more Is have a similar effect, although not as severe. Love and compassion shown to others during these transits eases any difficulties.

THE DAILY FORECAST

We have now calculated the main numbers used in a numerological forecast. It is not a question of analysing one number but of combining accurately the effect of many. Most of our days are a

THE EVENT NUMBER

The Event Number shows the essence, or the combined likely effect, of your current Transiting Letters. The numbers of these Transiting Letters are added together (fadically). For instance: A(1), R(9), and K(2) would give an Event Number of 3; H(8) and X(7) would give an Event Number of 6.

The Event Number and the Letters of Transit are analysed together.

Event Number 1: New beginnings. New starts. A fresh direction. An opportunity to start anew.

Event Number 2: Cooperation and partnerships. A quiet time. An opportunity to make friends.

Event Number 3: Life becomes joyful. A happy social period. An opportunity to be creative.

Event Number 4: Hard work and self-discipline. A practical period. An opportunity to achieve stability or put down roots.

Event Number 5: Surprising changes. Freedom is sought. Communication enhanced. An opportunity to try something new.

Event Number 6: Responsibilities taken on. Creativity is expressed. An opportunity to achieve a well-balanced life.

Event Number 7: Inner knowledge gained. Study and meditation enhanced. An opportunity to find your spiritual path. Unlooked for victories.

Event Number 8: Goals can be reached. Rewards arrive if deserved. An opportunity to become more independent.

Event Number 9: Emotional period. Something ends. Idealistic time. An opportunity to gain understanding.

mishmash of emotions and events and our daily numbers usually reflect this. Occasionally the same number is repeated many times in a forecast – this indicates an important period – the qualities this number represents will determine the likely outcome of the day (or month, and so on).

A quick way to find the daily vibrations is to calculate the Universal Day, then find your Personal Day by adding your Goal Number to the Universal. The Universal Day shows the help you can get from others; the Personal Day shows what you can do to help yourself.

For instance: Universal Day 1, Personal Day 7 – good for initiating new projects with outside help but you may prefer to spend time alone thinking how to perfect your plans/life. If you should decide to act, the outcome could be successful in a materialistic sense (1 and 7

THE PREDICTIVE NUMBERS

Life Path 5   Universal Day 5

Cycle 7   Universal Month 9

Challenge 5   Universal Year 3

Turning Point 0

Personal Day 8

Personal Year 6

Personal Month 3

Transit Letter S(1)

Transit Letter Z(8)

Transit Letter G(7)

Event Number 7

added together make 8). For more detailed analysis you will need to write down all your predictive numbers. Include your Life Path for guidance. Here is one particular day for a man with a 5 Life Path:

At first glance this may look like a bewildering list of numbers. The important consideration is how these numbers affect the Life Path Number. The Life Path Number and Universal Day Number are both 5. This is an excellent day for this person to pursue his personal ambitions. The world is in accord with him. His Personal Day being 8 shows he will need to set goals or strive ahead (5 and 8, while conflicting, are a dynamic combination). This is probably a purposeful day for him.

The following subtle vibrations affect his life over a longer period: the Universal Numbers, all being odd numbers, are harmonious with his Life Path; so also is his Personal Month. However, it is probably not an easy year for him as his Personal Year is 6 – responsibilities and domestic concerns will not necessarily harmonise well with his 5 Life Path.

His Cycle and Event Number are the deeply mysterious 7; he will think a lot about his personal motives during this period. The 7 vibration has a calming effect on the 5 but is harmonious.

Unfortunately, this Cycle has a 5 Challenge behind it and he will find it harder to follow the dictates of his Life Path. He will find this easier to conquer as he ages. The period is good financially (G and Z) and some form of surprising change (the S) is quite likely to occur during the year.

The overall look of this list is somewhat scattered, but this month should be lucky for him if he needs help from other people (Life Path 5, Universal Year 3, Universal Month 9 – all numbers that are in reasonable harmony).

The 7 Event Number coming in a 7 Cycle suggests that the birthday year (from birthday to birthday) is important, if in a quiet and understated way.

THE COMPLETE
NUMEROLOGY PROFILE

CHAPTER THIRTEEN

Life consists not in holding good cards
but in playing those you do hold well.

JOSH BILLINGS

You have discovered all your important numbers. They may appear to form a complex pattern. Everyone is not simply 'a 2' or 'a 6', just as they are not simply a Taurean or a Leo. You may have one or two numbers that dominate your chart; this makes it easier to analyse.

> ### PUT TOGETHER ALL YOUR NUMBERS
> ### BY MAKING A LIST IN THIS ORDER:
>
> | | | |
> |---|---|---|
> | 1 Life Path | 7 Consonant Number | 14 Last Letter |
> | 2 Birthchart | 8 Name Number | 15 Intensity |
> | 3 Lines on the | 9 Power | 16 Missing Numbers |
> | Birthchart | 10 First Name Number | 17 Namechart |
> | 4 Birthday | 11 First Letter | 18 Submerged |
> | 5 Goal | 12 First Vowel | Characteristic |
> | 6 Vowel Number | 13 Middle Letter | 19 Temperament Chart |

The charts of the Birthchart, Namechart and Temperament Chart can be placed on a separate piece of paper but keep the names on the list.

From your first number (your Life Path) work your way down the list (consulting the charts when you need to), analysing your strengths and weaknesses as you go. It is important you compare all your numbers and numerological patterns to how they relate to your Life Path Number. Do you have an easy or difficult chart? What areas need attention?

You may prefer to only list the main numbers (as set out in chapter 10) and this can be less confusing. The main numbers are: Life Path; Birthday; Goal; Name Number; Vowel Number; Consonant Number; First Name Number; Power; First Letter, First Vowel; and Intensity.

After studying the above numbers, you can forecast any trends occurring in your life by listing your numbers of prediction. As we discovered (in chapters 11 and 12) they are: your present Cycle; Challenge; Turning Point (if in operation); the Universal Year; Universal Month; Universal Day; Personal Year; Personal Month; Personal Day; Letters of Transit; and the current Event Number.

As an example we will look at the numbers of a legend: Marilyn Monroe. She was born June 1st 1926 (6 + 1 + 1926 = 25, 2 + 5 = 7).

NUMEROLOGY PROFILE: MARILYN MONROE

LIFE PATH 7

She was an individualist, needing time to herself each day. The 7 learns by experience and makes its own mistakes. It dislikes working as part of a team. To those who knew her, her solitariness was a notable trait that is quoted in many biographies. She once said: 'I would like to be more sociable than I am.' This describes the holder of a 7 Life Path Number well but is far from her public image: the entertaining dumb blonde. But her image appears (accurately) in her Consonant Number (see p.116).

THE COMPLETE NUMEROLOGY PROFILE

<table>
<tr><td></td><td>**6 6**</td><td>9</td></tr>
<tr><td>2</td><td></td><td></td></tr>
<tr><td>**1 1**</td><td></td><td></td></tr>
</table>

LEFT MARILYN MONROE'S BIRTHCHART .

Two 1s: Expressive. Effective position for working in the public eye.

One 2: Perceptive and emotionally sensitive.

Missing 3: A fear of using creative expression.

Missing 4: Lacked practicality, careless over routine details.

Missing 5: Needing someone to motivate her.

Two 6s: Creative. Harmonious. Home-life was important: a foster child who needed a secure home environment. This need would stay with her. It is at odds with her 7 Life Path which is not a domestic number. Conflicting domestic needs would occur in her life.

Missing 7: Dislike of being alone – this was negated by her 7 Life Path.

Missing 8: Carelessness and laziness over organization.

One 9: Of little significance; representing idealism common to everyone born at this time.

LINES ON BIRTHCHART

Missing 3-5-7: Encourages nervousness. She would have been either extremely sceptical or welcoming of new ideas. Probably the latter.

BIRTHDAY 1

Leadership and a dislike of taking orders. Original people. With her 7 Life Path this created a strong individualistic streak. Her own concerns and needs would dominate her life

GOAL 7

She aimed to achieve self-knowledge, to be comfortable with herself when alone. Her three main birth numbers were 7 1 7 – creating a powerful individuality. The 7 is not always an easy number – making things unnecessarily difficult for itself at times; sometimes it will sacrifice everything to have its own way. From her birth numbers this is not someone who would be easily manipulated. She would know what she wanted.

NAME CHART

Marilyn Monroe was enrolled at her school as Norma Jean Baker and it is likely this is the main spelling she used until she married her first husband at sixteen, Jim Dougherty. Recent biographers have chosen to spell Jean with an 'e' (Jeane) as she sometimes spelt it like this and it is the correct spelling on her birth certificate. What name she used consistently is a grey area. There are at least eight, possibly ten, names at various times. For the famous nude calendar she modelled under the name Mona Monroe. As Marilyn Monroe she left her past behind so this is the name we will examine.

VOWEL NUMBER 7

This is a perfect complement to her 7 Life Path. She would have welcomed her Life Path opportunities. It reinforces the need for privacy that we see in the birth numbers. She kept her thoughts, her real needs, to herself. Seven has deep emotional needs but has difficulty in communicating them. This number helps the intuition develop and has a need to taste the experiences life has to offer.

CONSONANT NUMBER 3

Her public persona was different from the numbers we have examined so far. Here is the bright, scintillating 3 of the entertainer. Gregarious, the life of the party, someone who communicates fun, happiness and joy as a first impression. This would have been the first public image. Different from the 7, it is still – being an odd number – in harmony.

NAME NUMBER I

The name, Marilyn Monroe, is harmonious with her 7 Life Path. The Name Number is also in harmony with her Vowel and Consonant Numbers. As Marilyn Monroe she would make her way through life in an original way.

The stress in her life (Life Path 7 subtracted from Name Number 1 = 6) would have shown up in her domestic life: a stress that is also shown between her Life Path and the two 6s on her Birthchart. Domestic harmony would have been difficult to keep hold of – as shown in her three marriages. This stress would have been compounded by her 1 Birthday, another number that does not fit well with domesticity.

POWER 8

Her Life Path 7 and Name Number 1 added together create the number 8. A powerful combination. Ambition, originality, individualism and goal-setting are all combined. Striving unflinchingly towards career success is the usual manifestation of this number.

If for a moment we stop using fadic addition, we then have a Life Path number of 25 and a Name Number of 73; add them together, again not using fadic addition, and we are left with a Power Number of 98. The following words total 98: 'Film Star' and 'Renowned' – this was the power that was easier to gain when she changed her name from Norma Jean Baker to Marilyn Monroe. Her 7 Life Path, striving to achieve perfection, enabled her to improve her acting by an intensive study of the 'method' school. The 7 here would not be satisfied by material success alone.

FIRST NAME NUMBER 2

In her private life she would want a partner or companion. She probably felt some conflict here as her real needs for self-examination and solitude were suppressed. There is a big difference between the private and public aspects of this name.

FIRST LETTER M(4)

Encourages practicality, integrity and mood changes. Desires love and excitement.

FIRST VOWEL A(1)

Her first emotional reaction would have been assertive, taking action on her needs.

MIDDLE LETTER I(9)

Dramatic and romantic feelings could have become obsessive.

LAST LETTER N(5)

Affairs would have been concluded in an unpredictable way. A need for change.

INTENSITY 9 & 5

In Marilyn Monroe the strongest numbers are: 9, compassion, romance, idealism; and 5, communication, seeking change and freedom, plus sexuality.

MISSING NUMBERS 2 & 8

The 2 is on her Birthchart, so it does not count. She had the 8 as her Power Number, which would have helped develop some organizational skills and financial acumen. The 3 and 7 missing on her Birthchart are contained in her name.

NAMECHART

Marilyn Monroe on this chart complements and balances her Birthchart. Try it and see. The 8 is still missing but she now has it as her Power Number.

SUBMERGED CHARACTERISTIC 4

This number helped her to bring a practical and orthodox approach into play when she needed to.

MARILYN MONROE'S TEMPERAMENT CHART

MENTAL 4: The name promoted logical thinking.

PHYSICAL 3: Life was faced in an artistic way.

EMOTIONAL 5: Emotional change was assisted.

INTUITIVE 1: Ideas would appear suddenly, creatively.

There are many letters on the Start line, giving good ability to create and no difficulty in continuing. Perhaps a need to try harder to finish projects at times.

SUMMARY

It is likely that for her first sixteen years she was known as Norma Jean (without an e) Baker. This spelling of Norma Jean was used by two husbands, appeared on her first wedding invitation and was used by the woman who looked after her for her first eight years. Marilyn Monroe was created four years later. Here, we will briefly compare Norma Jean Baker to Marilyn Monroe.

When we look at her important numbers (as in the suggested list in chapter 10) we see that as Norma Jean Baker, the dominant number was the number 1 (occurring five times) with 5 and 7 appearing twice. As 7 was her Life Path, 1 and 7 would have been her two most important numbers. With so many 1s it would have been difficult for her not to over-emphasize the qualities of her 1 Birthday instead of those of her 7 Life Path.

For someone born June 1st 1926 the important numbers of the name Marilyn Monroe achieve a better balance than Norma Jean Baker. Her most repeated numbers are 1 and 7 (both appearing three times) and she had a single number under every digit except the number 6; although 1 and 7 occur the same number of times, the 7s contain her Life Path. Seven becomes her strongest number. A fortunate occurrence. Her own free will would decide how she would ultimately act in life but the change in name made it easier for her to follow her true desires.

PREDICTIVE NUMBERS

For her Letters of Transit and Event Numbers we use the name as written on her birth certificate. This is Baby Norma Jeane Mortenson. It was not necessary to write the word baby but it has been written down. Some numerologists would consider this divine guidance. Her mother's name Mortensen, has a different spelling (the vowels) than the version of it officially placed on Norma Jeane's birth certificate. But it is the official version, with mistakes and extraneous words, that is always used.

It is a confusing chart, but symbolically her first Event Number is a 3: the mark of the entertainer.

Only during three years in her entire life did she not have a Transiting Letter that did not represent the number 5. Five, the number of communication, freedom, and often associated with sexuality, was present for thirty-three of her thirty-six years. When we look at her First Challenge, we see it was also 5. Not only did life continuously bring her opportunities related to the five senses, but until the age of twenty-nine she would have needed to overcome the problems they represent. People with 5 dominant often attract occurrences that have a basis (if unconscious) in their sexuality.

Her First Cycle (to twenty-nine years) was a 6. There would have been the need for a secure home ever-present. She was brought up in various foster homes and an orphanage (which one could not forecast from numerology) but although the 6 Cycle would create a desire for 'domestic bliss', it conflicts with the 1s and 7s in her chart. Her Life Path 7 shows someone who is essentially a loner, whatever the other numbers say, and Marilyn Monroe's other numbers reinforce the individualism of the 7 and leadership of the 1.

Her predictive chart is not especially easy. Twenty-four of her years she had two or more of the same letters transiting. This can create too strong an effect and bring out the negative qualities of the numbers that are involved.

She married at an early age the son of a neighbour, Jim Dougherty. This was during a 5 Personal Year and one could speculate that it was a way for her to seek freedom. She had a 7 Event Number, the Universal Year was 7, and she was sixteen years old – 16, a fadic 7. The 7 of her Life Path keeps appearing at significant occasions in her life. Four years later, during a 9 Personal Year (endings), she divorced him in Las Vegas.

MARILYN MONROE'S BIG DAY

The most important day in her life was July 16th 1946. She walked into the office of Ben Lyon, who was chief talent scout at Twentieth Century-Fox. He is reported to have looked at her and said: 'Honey, you're in pictures.'

The day was the 16th – a 7; the month was July – a 7; the Universal Day (7. 16. 1946) was a 7; her Personal Month was a 7. Her lucky number repeated four times combined with the ending of her old life as reflected in the number 9: her Personal Year was 9; her Event Number was 9; the Universal Month was 9. The numbers 7, 7, 7, 7, and 9, 9, 9, combined with the freedom-seeking 5 of her Personal Day. Within fourteen days she had a seven-year film contract, a new name, new image and new life. She was about to become a 'film star' – a word seen in her new Power Number. She became Marilyn Monroe.

That ever-imitated photograph of her – standing over an air-vent on the sidewalk, white dress billowing around her waist – is from arguably her most famous film 'The *Seven* Year Itch'. The film title also totals a fadic 7. Production of the film was stopped on a 7 Universal

Day; and the première was just after her First Turning Point, another 7, came into force.

To select briefly some important events: in 1953 she received the 'Photoplay Gold Medal', at the time a prestigious award. She was in a 7 Personal Year with a 7 Event Number in transit.

She formed her own production company at the age of 27 in the same 7 Personal Year but with an 8 Event Number now in transit. Eight, the natural number of the executive and business world.

In 1956, after fighting the infamous studio system she returned on her own terms, now a powerful figure in possession of an impressive contract. She was in a 1 Personal Year (new starts); the start also of a 1 Cycle; a 4 Event Number may seem limiting but here it had the powerful full number of 22 (considered a Master Number) behind it (masterful achievements); and her First Turning Point was now activated – a 7.

In June of the same year she married the playwright, Arthur Miller – himself a Life Path 7. In later life President Kennedy is reported to have been a friend – another 7 Life Path.

She died during a 7 Personal Year at the age of 36 in mysterious (a word often associated with the number 7) circumstances. Her death was reported to the police in the early hours of August 5th 1962. Intriguingly, her grandmother, Della Hogan Monroe, was committed to a mental institution 35 years earlier (7 fives make 35) on August 4th 1927 – a 4 Universal Day. As Marilyn died the Universal Day was 4 and she had a 4 Event Number in force. Numerology cannot predict death, and the calendar number of the day seems more fitting for the departure of a 'sex goddess' – a 5.

When we understand our motivation and our desires we are poised to achieve greater fulfilment in our lives. Numerology is a traditionally based system that can help achieve this. There are others. I hope you find the knowledge held within numbers gives you the key to open many doors.

May your counting be correct and your numbers lucky.

RECOMMENDED READING

Blackwell Lawrence, Shirley, *Behind Numerology*, Newcastle Publishing Co, North Hollywood, 1989.

Campbell, Florence, *Your Days are Numbered*, DeVorss & Co, Marina Del Rey, 1987.

Konraad, Sandor, *Numerology: Key to the Tarot*, Whitford Press, West Chester, 1983.

Line, Julia, *The Numerology Workbook*, The Aquarian Press, Wellingborough, 1985.

Phillips, Dr David A., *Secrets of the Inner Self*, Angus & Robertson, Australia & London, 1981.

BIBLIOGRAPHY

Anderson, Marr, *Numerology: The Secret Power of Numbers*, Aquarian Press, Wellingborough, 1979.

Andrews, Ted, *The Magical Name*, Liewellyn Publications, St Paul, MN, 1991.

Andrews, Ted, *The Sacred Power in Your Name*, Liewellyn Publications, St Paul, MN, 1990.

Bek, Lilla and Holden, Robert, *What Number Are You?*, Aquarian Press, London, 1992.

Bernstein, Henrietta, *Cabalah Primer*, DeVorss & Co, Marina Del Rey, 1984.

Bishop, Barbara J., *Numerology: The Universal Vibrations of Numbers*, Liewellyn Publications, St Paul, 1990.

Bosman, Leonard, *The Meaning and Philosophy of Numbers*, Rider & Co, London, 1932.

Buess, Lynn M., *Numerology for the New Age*, DeVorss & Co, Marina Del Rey, 1987.

Bunker, Dusty, *Numerology and Your Future*, Para Research, West Chester, 1987.

Cheiro, *Cheiro's Book of Numbers*, Prentice Hall, New York, 1988.

Coates, Austin, *Numerology*, Granada Publishing, London, 1978.

Cooper D. Jason, *Understanding Numerology*, The Aquarian Press, Wellingborough, 1990.

Culbert, S.J., *Your Lucky Number*, W. Foulsham & Co, London, 1986.

Culbert, Steven John, *The Right Name for Baby*, W Fonlsham & Co, 1988.

Davies, Rodney, *Fortune Telling with Numbers*, The Aquarian Press, Wellingborough, 1986.

Eisen, William, *The Cabalah of Astrology*, DeVorss & Co, Marina Del Rey, 1986.

Godwin, Joscelyn, *The Mystery of the Seven Vowels*, Phanes Press, Grand Rapids, 1991.

Goodman, Morris C., *Modern Numerology*, Fleet Press Corporation, New York, 1945.

Goodwin, Mathew Oliver, *Numerology: The Complete Guide*, Vols 1 & 2, Newcastle Publishing Co, North Hollywood, 1981.

Gruner, Mark, and Brown, Christopher K., *Numbers of Life*, Taplinger Publishing Co, New York, 1978.

Hitchcock, Helyn, *Helping Yourself with Numerology*, Wolfe Publishing Ltd., London, 1972.

Hoffstein, Robert M., *A Mystical Key to the English Language*, Destiny Books, Rochester, 1992.

Jam, Manik Chand, *Birthday Numerology*, Sagar Publications, New Delhi, 1973.

Javane, Faith, *Master Numbers: Cycles of Divine Order*, Whitford Press, West Chester, 1988.

Javane, Faith, and Bunker, Dusty, *Numerology and The Divine Triangle*, Whitford Press, West Chester, 1979.

Johari, Harish, *Numerology: With Tantra, Ayurveda and Astrology*, Destiny Books, Rochester, 1990.

Jordan, Juno, *Numerology, The Romance in Your Name*, DeVorss & Co, Marina Del Rey, 1978.

Kiley, Shirlee and Gordon, Rochelle, *Your Name is Your Destiny*, Pan Books, London, 1984.

Kumar, Ravindra, *Secrets of Numerology*, Sterling Publishers, New Delhi, 1992.

Le Gette, Bernard Spencer, *Numera: The Craft of Numerology*, Pan Books, London, 1976.

Rael, Joseph E. and Sutton, Lindsay, *Tracks of Dancing Light*, Element Books Ltd, Shaftesbury, 1993.

Rice, Paul and Valeta, *Potential: The Name Analysis Book*, Samuel Weiser Inc., York Beach, 1987.

Sachs, Bob, *The Complete Guide to Nine Star Ki*, Element Books Ltd, Shaftesbury, 1992.

Sepharial, *Kabalistic Astrology*, Newcastle Publishing Co, North Hollywood, 1981.

Seton, Julia, *Western Symbology*, The Rally, London, 1933.

Stebbing, Lionel, *The Secrets of Numbers*, New Knowledge Books, Sussex, 1963.

Stein, Robin, *Your Child's Numerology*, Futura Publications, London & Sydney, 1987.

Stein, Sandra Kovacs, *Instant Numerology*, Newcastle Publishing Co, North Hollywood, 1985.

Stein, Sandra Kovacs and Schuler, Carol Ann, *Love Numbers*, Sphere Books Ltd, London, 1982.

Strayhom, Lloyd, *Numbers and You*, Ballantine Books, New York, 1987.

Ariel Yvon, *Numerology Made Plain*, Newcastle Publishing Co, 1973.

Taylor, Ariel Yvon and Hyer, H. Warren, *Numerology: Its Facts and Secrets*, Sagar Publications, New Delhi, 1973.

Tono, Helen, *It All Adds Up To Love*, Bantam Books, London, 1989.

Valla, Mary, *The Power of Numbers*, DeVorss & Co, California, 1985.

Vaughan, Richard, *Numbers as Symbols for Self-discovery*, CRCS Publications, Sebastopol, 1973.

Young, Ellin Dodge and Schuler, Carol Ann, *The Vibes Book*, Samuel Weiser, New York, 1979.

INDEX

action 36
alphabet 48, 68–76,
    85–91, 105–9
ambition 23–4, 65,
    74
    name analysis
        50, 51, 56, 63

birthchart 25–38,
    115
birthdate
    see also
        birthchart; life
        path number
    cycles of life
        93–7
birthday number
    39–46

challenge number
    96–7, 114
communication
    20–1, 66
    cycles 95, 97
    life path number
        20–1
    name analysis
        62, 78
compassion 37, 41,
    66
    life path number
        24
    name analysis
        52, 57, 63, 79

conflict 52, 57, 64,
    91
consonant number
    53–9
contemplation
    22–3, 56, 63, 84
cooperation 41, 58,
    65, 69, 87
    life path number
        17–18
    name analysis
        43, 54, 61, 78
creativity
    66, 70, 88
    birthchart
        number 29, 31
    birthdays 40, 41,
        44
    life path number
        18–19, 21–2,
        24
    name analysis
        55, 57, 62, 78,
        80, 84
cycles of life 93–7,
    114

day 100–2, 114
determination
    16–17, 40, 54, 65
    birthcharts 28,
        30, 37
diplomacy 17–18,
    65

name analysis
    54, 61, 78, 83
domesticity 21–2,
    31–2, 89, 97
    birthdays 42, 44
    name analysis
        51, 56, 63
drama 24, 66

eccentricity
    38, 74
emotion 36,
    41, 43, 68
emotional letters
    69–76, 85–91
entertainment
    18–19, 65
event number 110,
    114

fadic addition 16
financial acumen
    42, 44, 71, 79, 81
first name number
    66–7
forecasting
    109–12
freedom 20–1, 30,
    43, 66, 70
    name analysis
        62, 78
friendship 17–18,
    44, 71
frustration 37

127